THE SECRETS OF SUCCESSFUL STRATEGIC ACCOUNT MANAGEMENT

How Industrial Sales Organizations Can Boost Revenue Growth and Profitability, Prevent Revenue Loss, and Convert Customers to Valued Partners

RICHARD SANTUCCI
AND DAVID HUGHES

THE SECRETS OF SUCCESSFUL STRATEGIC ACCOUNT MANAGEMENT
HOW INDUSTRIAL SALES ORGANIZATIONS CAN BOOST REVENUE GROWTH AND PROFITABILITY, PREVENT REVENUE LOSS, AND CONVERT CUSTOMERS TO VALUED PARTNERS

iUniverse books may be ordered through booksellers or by contacting:

iUniverse
1663 Liberty Drive
Bloomington, IN 47403
www.iuniverse.com
844-349-9409

Because of the dynamic nature of the Internet, any web addresses or links contained in this book may have changed since publication and may no longer be valid. The views expressed in this work are solely those of the author and do not necessarily reflect the views of the publisher, and the publisher hereby disclaims any responsibility for them.

Any people depicted in stock imagery provided by Getty Images are models, and such images are being used for illustrative purposes only.
Certain stock imagery © Getty Images.

ISBN: 978-1-6632-3479-7 (sc)
ISBN: 978-1-6632-3478-0 (e)

Library of Congress Control Number: 2022900524

Print information available on the last page.

iUniverse rev. date: 04/19/2022

Contents

Preface

Authors Richard Santucci and David Hughes accumulated over fifty years of experience in the industrial business-to-business (B2B) sales function with specific emphasis in sales management, distribution, and sales channeling strategies; marketing; strategic planning; sales resource onboarding and training; customer segmentation tactics; and in the last decade, strategic account management programing.

Their careers provide insights not found in academic treatises that are valuable to those involved in sales. Their trajectory in sales is rich in successes but also a few failures that collectively provide lessons learned through trial and error, illustrating what works and what does not. Realizing their experiences could bring value to current and future sales leaders, they decided to form S&H Strategic Sales Consulting, LLC.

The sales discipline is a crucial, yet significantly broad company organizational function. As such, it cannot be covered in a holistic manner. So, they decided to first write about their knowledge in strategic account management programming. They hope this work guides sales leaders through the organizational process and more importantly, brings tangible value to your bottom line.

Introduction:
The Burning Platform for
Strategic Account Management

It is true, especially as it relates to industrial companies, that a large percentage of a company's business is transacted by a small percentage of its customers. Anecdotally, it is often said that 80 percent of an industrial company's business is provided by 20 percent of its current customers. Many of those customers should be considered strategic accounts and provided with enhanced attention and resources.

The following fictitious, but very possible, scenario illustrates the importance of understanding who your strategic accounts are and making sure that you assign the necessary resources to keep them as your most important customers.

Imagine that you are a manufacturer of high-end widgets. Your company is called Dynamic Corporation. Acme Corporation is one of the 20 percent of Dynamic's customers providing 80 percent of its business. In fact, Acme is responsible for almost 8 percent of Dynamic's annual sales.

John Smith, a sales representative with Dynamic Corporation, has called on the Acme location in Hometown, Montana, for ten years. John knows all the key people at the Hometown location and has a great relationship with all of them. The employees at Hometown love John. They are incredibly happy with his service and the performance of the widgets his company manufactures. One beautiful summer day, John visits the Hometown location, making his normal monthly visit, only to be told that they will no longer be buying widgets from Dynamic Corporation. When he asks why, he is told that the decision was made by the corporate headquarters in New York City.

John, of course, is upset about this turn of events and does some further due diligence. First, he asks his VP of sales, Larry Wilson, who it is that is assigned to call on Acme's corporate headquarters in New York. To his surprise, he is told that since the corporate headquarters does not actually place any orders for widgets, no one is assigned to call on that location. John then calls the procurement leader at Acme to understand why the decision was made to purchase from someone else. He finds out that Globex Corporation has been calling on Acme's headquarters for quite some time and made them a proposal to provide all the widgets for all their global locations for an attractive price. Further, he finds that several of Acme's locations in China were experiencing delivery issues with Dynamic's widgets coming from their factory in Asia. After evaluating Globex's widgets technically and feeling comfortable with their supply chain capability and financial capacity, they decided to switch all their business to Globex Corporation.

Just like that, with one decision 8 percent of Dynamic's business is gone! This could have been prevented had Dynamic employed a strategic account management program that would have focused a significant effort on making sure that the value proposition of Dynamic's widgets was made clear to the employees at Acme's headquarters and would have monitored threats that could possibly put the business at risk. Ensuring that major customers like Acme Corporation do not make unilateral decisions like this one is one of the main reasons for having a strategic account program.

This book explains why a customer like the Acme Corporation should have been included in a strategic account management program and how that program could have avoided the significant loss of their business. We begin by defining strategic account management and its major benefits. Then once a decision is made to embark on a strategic account program, there are a number of processes that need to be followed to ensure the program's success. We go on to explain in detail those critical processes, beginning with account selection and ending with creating a communication plan. We will take you through the chapters utilizing the following flowchart where we highlight each topic as we move from one chapter to the next. Throughout the book we have included helpful tools. These are all included in the appendices at the end of the book. So, let's get started on our journey to boost revenue growth and profitability, prevent revenue loss, and convert customers to valued partners through strategic account management!

Strategic Account Management Process

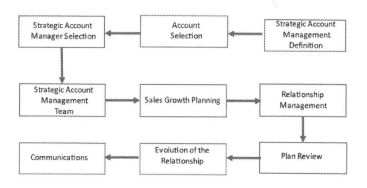

CHAPTER ONE
Strategic Account Management Definition and Benefits

Strategic Account Management Process

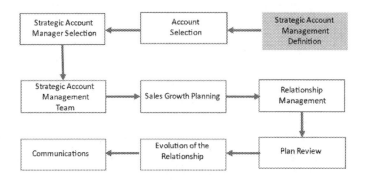

What Is Strategic Account Management?

No doubt there is not one definition of strategic account management. However, after years of running a program for several companies, we like the following definition:

> Strategic account management is **an enterprise-wide initiative** to develop strategic relationships with **a limited number of customers** in order to achieve long-term, sustained, significant, and **measurable business value for both the strategic account and your company.**

Let us focus on a few of the phrases in the above definition that are the keys to a successful strategic account program.

First, "an enterprise-wide initiative." It is especially important that all parts of the organization understand and participate in the strategic account program. In short, it is *not* just a sales program. Marketing, manufacturing, finance, and legal must all participate to some extent in supporting each strategic account. Marketing can contribute by providing important collateral that can help explain to the strategic account the value of the overall program and understand the customer's strategy to win in the context of their industry. In fact, a new trend is developing whereby marketing is assigning an account-based marketeer to the strategic account management program. Finance can contribute by providing important financial information that will help the account manager decide the correct resources to expend on each account. Manufacturing can contribute by understanding the global needs of the strategic account and by leveraging supply chain resources to meet those needs. And legal can contribute by helping the account team navigate the negotiation of global contracts.

Second, "a limited number of customers." When launching a strategic account program, some companies make the mistake of assigning too many accounts to the program and then not resourcing it properly. This can lead to a program that is not impactful to the strategic account as resources become diluted. We suggest a company start with only those customers that are most strategic to the company's business. It is always easier to add accounts to the program than to eliminate them.

Third, "measurable business value for both the strategic account and your company." This is quite clear but particularly important. The strategic account program must provide measurable value to the strategic account and the company running the program, or it will not be beneficial and will typically receive little attention in the way of resources. The strategic account must view the program as helping it be successful in some way. It could be that the program improves the strategic account's profit by providing innovative solutions that reduce overall cost to the business. Or it could be that the company provides resources that help the account increase productivity. Whatever the benefit or benefits, it must be clear and demonstrable to the strategic account.

Likewise, the company must also see a benefit. Many times, this benefit takes the form of an increase in business from the strategic account in exchange for valuable resources directed toward the account.

Later we look more specifically at how each of these factors can be addressed in more detail.

What Are the Benefits of a Strategic Account Program?

While companies can list many benefits of launching and running a strategic account program, we believe that the major benefits are in four areas.

First, growth. There is an organization focused specifically on sharing best practices related to strategic account management called SAMA (Strategic Account Management Association). SAMA conducts a robust survey of its members on a periodic basis. One of the survey questions frequently asked is how much growth the members have seen by customers that are part of their strategic account program versus those that are not part of the program. From figure 1, you can see that the revenue growth provided by those accounts in the strategic account program was much more significant than those customers outside the program. These are exactly the type of results that we would expect and frankly demand that a company derives from a strategic account program.

In short, in times of economic growth, a company should expect their strategic accounts to grow at a more significant rate than those accounts outside the program. Likewise, in times of economic decline, a company should expect that the revenue from strategic accounts will decline less than revenue from accounts not in the program. While there are other reasons for implementing a strategic account program, this is by far the most important. In fact, we would argue that if your strategic account program does not lead to more significant revenue or profit growth, the expense of the program is probably not justified.

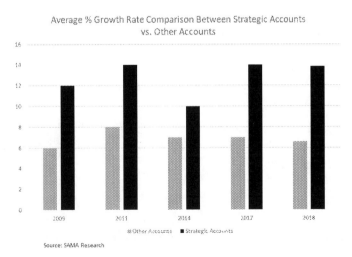

Source: SAMA Research

Figure 1

4

Second, risk mitigation. We saw in our fictitious scenario that it is possible to lose a significant amount of business very quickly when companies, like Acme, make global, unilateral decisions. Given the current trend by companies to centralize decision-making, especially around procurement/commodity management, if a supplier is not paying attention to the corporate relationship with a major customer by way of a skilled strategic account manager, that company runs the risk of losing business very quickly. The global account manager and the manager's team are responsible for addressing issues that are being dealt with by the customer's corporate team, so those issues do not become a reason for terminating the relationship. Many issues can lead to the termination of a relationship. Following are a few of them:

- Late delivery of product or service
- Poor customer service at customer locations
- Poor product quality
- Lack of product or service co-creation
- Lack of engineering/technical support
- Inability to provide consistent product quality, service, or commercial offering across the enterprise

Any one of these issues can lead to a customer deciding to leave a current supplier for another. It is the responsibility of the strategic account manager and his or her team to address these issues quickly, so they do not lead to a decision by the customer to end the relationship. In addressing and resolving any of the issues listed previously, the strategic account team not only mitigates the risk of losing the customer's business but, more importantly eliminates a major problem for the customer.

Third, account trends toward centralization. Over the

past decade, we have seen a movement toward centralized decision-making in large corporations, especially as it is related to procurement. In fact, the commodity management organizations within many major companies did not even exist in the twentieth century but now can be quite significant and wield significant power. In many cases, they are responsible for negotiating global contracts that can be utilized at locations across the enterprise. In doing so, they leverage the companies' global spend to obtain the best commercial and technical deal. Commodity managers expect to have a single person, or a single team, negotiate these agreements, so the account and the company can become aligned on both commercial and technical terms. This can be exceedingly difficult when a company does not have a strategic account organization. Companies whose sales teams are organized mainly geographically may find that the sales team that resides in the region where the customer's corporate location exists is hesitant to put forth the effort necessary to negotiate such an agreement when they may only receive limited benefits. For example, if a company headquartered in Europe does most of its business in the Middle East, the sales team in Europe may not want to expend the effort to negotiate a global deal when the Middle East will benefit most. There is also the additional complexity of getting internal alignment with all the sales regions and other company departments that will be critical in making any agreement successful.

The negotiation of these agreements thus becomes the responsibility of the strategic account team led by the strategic account manager. The account manager and the manager's team essentially represent all departments of the company and negotiate on their behalf. Once an agreement is in place, the account manager monitors the agreement activity and is responsible for reporting on the status of the agreement, as well as working with the account leaders to make any necessary changes.

While the negotiation of global contracts is a critical responsibility of the account team, the strategic account manager, in general, is responsible for the overall corporate relationship with the account. This means maintaining clear two-way communication between all engaged departments within the account and the company.

In summary, we feel that an important account whose decision-making is mainly centralized is a prime candidate for a strategic account effort. The company and the account can realize significant benefits from this.

Fourth, strategic account industry influence. In any market there are always leading companies, companies who lead the way in methodology, process, and technology. As examples, in the energy business, one might think of ExxonMobil or Chevron as leaders and in the chemical business, BASF or Dow. If these are indeed leading companies, this means that others in the industry usually follow. So, for a company that provides products or services to ExxonMobil, Chevron, BASF, or Dow, that company should be as close to these accounts as possible. If they decided to align themselves with a specific company because of a unique methodology, process, or technology, it is likely that many others in the industry will follow. And the best way to stay close to these accounts is by having a strategic account team that continually provides the account with potential solutions that will help them improve their businesses, solutions that can be leveraged to provide a benefit to the account across its entire network. Establishing an enterprise-wide initiative to develop strategic relationships with leading accounts in your particular industry can benefit both the accounts and your company.

While there are undoubtedly additional reasons for

establishing a strategic account program within your company, we believe the most compelling reasons are, as stated above, growth, risk mitigation, account trends toward centralization, and account industry influence.

Let us revisit our opening story in the introduction and assume that Dynamic Corporation had indeed established a strategic account program with an account manager, Jill Anderson, calling on Acme's corporate headquarters. What might the outcome look like then?

First, because Jill has a solid relationship with Acme's corporate leaders, she finds out about the delivery issues happening in China and is able to tap her enterprise team members to address the problem quickly and mitigate the risk related to the delivery issues for Acme. Second, since she has a relationship with Acme's corporate engineering team, which makes centralized technical decisions for all of Acme's locations, and she has a Dynamic engineering member as part of her virtual team, she is able to understand Acme's global technical needs and launch a project to cocreate a new line of widgets to address their specific requirements. This leads to an increase in business. Instead of losing all of Acme's business, they are able to grow its business by 20 percent in one year. And lastly, as a result of creating a new product to help Acme, several other specialty widget customers begin to buy the new widgets as well. So, all four reasons for putting a strategic account program in place materialize.

Now we review the critical processes involved in building and executing a strategic account program, beginning with account selection.

CHAPTER TWO
Selecting Strategic Accounts

Strategic Account Management Process

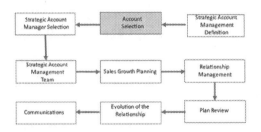

One of the most important activities related to any strategic account program is the account selection process. As we indicated in the last chapter, companies that are just beginning a strategic account effort should limit the number of initial accounts in the program. While there are many ways of selecting strategic accounts, we believe there should be a sound process using relevant criteria for doing so. Initially, it might seem clear which accounts should be selected first. Accounts that represent a significant amount of revenue would certainly seem to qualify to be a part of the program. In addition, accounts that are leaders in an industry that uses a significant amount of goods or services from a given company should be considered as strategic accounts. For example, a company that manufacturers subsea oil drilling equipment would probably want to have customers such as Chevron and ExxonMobil in their strategic account program. In many cases, the initial list of accounts that should participate in a strategic account program becomes obvious as they represent a significant amount of revenue, are clear leaders in their industries, and/or offer great growth potential for the future.

Regardless of how obvious the addition of some accounts might be to a strategic account program, it is good practice to establish a relatively robust selection process that uses both objective and subjective criteria to score multiple accounts and get an overall picture of which accounts should be part of the program and which accounts should not. When considering a selection process, the following should be addressed.

1. The selection matrix to be used to score potential accounts
2. The selection team involved in scoring the potential accounts
3. The rhythm established to review periodically the accounts in the strategic account program
4. The next steps to take once an account is selected or deselected from the program

The Selection Matrix

One of the best ways to select the accounts that will be the focus of a strategic account program is to create a selection matrix. A typical selection matrix, such as the example in figure 2, is comprised of the following.

- Selection criteria
- Criteria weighting
- Criteria scoring
- Scoring guidance
- Overall account score

Potential Strategic Account	Acme			
Criteria	Selection Weight	Account Score	Account Criteria Scores	Scoring Guidance
Global Presence	15	3	45	Presence in one region = 1, presence in two regions = 3, presence in three regions = 5
Current Revenue	15	5	75	<1MM Revenue = 1, 1–5MM = 3, >5MM = 5
Revenue Growth Trend (over five-year period)	15	5	75	0–3% growth = 1, 4–10% growth = 3, >10% growth = 5
Current Profitability	25	5	125	<20% GM = 1, 20–25% GM = 3, >25% GM = 5
Account Leadership	15	3	45	Industry follower = 1, industry leader = 3, strong industry leader = 5
Interest in a Partnering Relationship	15	3	45	Little interest = 1, some interest = 3, strong interest in partnering = 5
Overall Account Score	100		410	

Figure 2

Selection Criteria

The selection criteria are usually specific to the industry and/ or the company. As you can see above, this matrix indicates that an account's global reach is an important criterion, but that may not always be a factor in considering an account as a strategic customer. Each company beginning a strategic account program needs to decide which criteria are the most important for selection purposes. It is usually a good practice to poll several areas of the company to get sound ideas about selection criteria. Clearly sales should have input, but it might be important to get input from other departments such as marketing, customer service, manufacturing, and finance. The example above lists five key criteria for account scoring. Here is a more exhaustive list.

- Global presence
- Global footprint/locations
- Current revenue
- Revenue growth trend (next five years)
- Potential revenue
- Profitability
- Potential profitability
- Cost to serve the account
- Industry leadership
- Interest in a partnership or strategic relationship
- Potential repeat or aftermarket business

After receiving input from critical stakeholders, the strategic account team needs to make the final decision on which criteria to utilize to score potential strategic accounts.

Criteria Weighting

Once the selection criteria has been determined, it is necessary to decide how important each criteria or factor is. As indicated previously, it has been determined that current revenue and profitability are the two most important criteria and have thus each been given a 25 percent weight. Note that regardless of the number of factors or criteria, the weighting of all of those should add up to 100 percent.

Criteria Scoring

Criteria scoring is really simple math. The account score given to each potential account is multiplied by the selection weighting to come up with a criteria score.

Scoring Guidance

When developing a strategic account selection matrix, it is especially important to include clear guidance on how to score each criteria. As you can see above, guidance is provided for each criteria. Without this, each scorer will inevitably create his or her own rules related to each of the selection factors. As a result, overall scoring will be inconsistent.

Overall Account Score

Like criteria scoring, this is simple math. Once the criteria scoring is completed, those scores are added together, and the sum is the overall account score, in this case, 400. Given the 100 percent weighting, and the fact that in this case the highest possible score is 5 for any particular criteria, the maximum score for any account would be 500.

Scoring should be conducted by a number of people in the organization, which we will address next. All individual scores should be added together and divided by the number of people scoring in order to arrive at an average score for each account.

All those scores should be compared and a cutoff determined. There are no right or wrong answers as to which score is needed for an account to be selected. Much of this depends on how many accounts a company decides to have in its program. As we said in the last chapter, we caution companies not to begin a program with too many strategic accounts. In figure 3 you can see a hypothetical scoring chart. In this case, the company has decided to select accounts CO1, CO2, CO3, CO4, and CO5 (those accounts shaded in black) and to pass on the accounts shaded in gray. You will notice that they have selected all accounts with an overall score of 400 or greater. Since there is quite a big difference between the score given to CO5 and CO6, this cutoff seems to make sense. Please note, however, that as we said earlier, there are no right or wrong answers. And we suggest that the accounts not selected continue to be monitored as "incubator accounts," which can potentially be added to the program as things evolve.

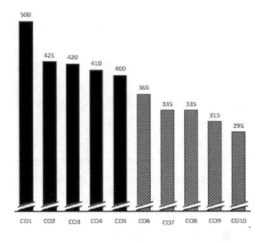

Figure 3

The Selection Team

As we indicated earlier, while the sales organization needs to have significant input in scoring and selecting strategic accounts, other parts of the organization should also provide input. We made it clear in chapter 1 that a successful strategic account program should be an enterprise-wide effort. This includes the initial and ongoing selection or deselection of accounts.

Each company needs to decide which departments will be involved in the strategic account effort, including the selection and deselection activities. In figure 4 we provide an example of an account selection committee chart. In this case, the company has included strategy/marketing, sales, service, manufacturing, engineering, and finance. The key stakeholders have been identified as well as their expected inputs. As you can see, their inputs, as would be expected, is related to their portions of the overall business. We would expect this to be the case if, for example, someone from customer service or IT was added as well to the selection committee.

The main point is that the decision around the selection of strategic accounts should be made with input from various parts of the company, not just sales. This is critically important in making a sound decision related to account selection. Case in point: Sales may want to select an account that represents a significant amount of revenue; finance may push back, pointing out that the customer returns an overall negative profit. Making a decision without input from finance, in this case, could lead to resources being focused on a customer who can provide little benefit to the company.

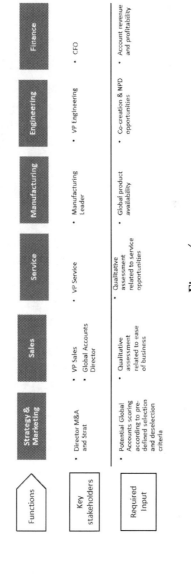

Global Account Selection & Deselection Committee

Functions	Strategy & Marketing	Sales	Service	Manufacturing	Engineering	Finance
Key stakeholders	• Director M&A and Strat	• VP Sales • Global Accounts Director	• VP Service	• Manufacturing Leader	• VP Engineering	• CFO
Required Input	• Potential Global Accounts scoring according to pre-defined selection and deselection criteria	• Qualitative assessment related to ease of business	• Qualitative assessment related to service opportunities	• Global product availability	• Co-creation & NPD opportunities	• Account revenue and profitability

Figure 4

Account Selection/Deselection Rhythm

When a company is just launching a strategic account program, it is necessary to create some type of selection tool, like the selection matrix provided in figure 2, and then decide who will be involved—the selection committee as depicted in figure 4—in scoring each account. Once the scoring is completed, a decision can be made as to which accounts should be included in the program, as shown in figure 3. However, as time progresses, things of course change. Strategic accounts may change their procurement strategies and demand price concessions that negatively impact the profitability of the accounts' businesses. Or they may decide that they no longer desire to have a strategic relationship with your company. As a result of these potential changes, as mentioned earlier, it is necessary to review all the accounts in the program periodically. We suggest that this be done once a year. This entails each stakeholder scoring each account again and having a formal selection team meeting to review the results of the account scores.

As in the initial selection process, this is not completely objective. In our experience, during these meetings and discussions there is always healthy debate related to certain accounts, and all input is welcomed. The goal is usually to arrive at a list of accounts on a consensus basis. If that is not possible, a disagreement can be resolved by vote. If the vote results in a tie, a decision for breaking the tie needs to be made. It might be the highest-ranking official who breaks the tie, or it could be the strategic account program leader. Regardless of how this is accomplished, it needs to be determined from the beginning and followed consistently.

While we recommend that this process takes place annually, it is possible that an event could occur that would make it necessary to select or deselect an account during the year. This recommendation is usually made by the strategic account manager or the overall program leader, but it could be made by any stakeholder. When this happens, a meeting of the selection committee needs to occur to discuss the reasons for the suggested change and decide whether to either retain or remove the account from the program.

Next Steps After Selection or Deselection

Selection

The actions to be taken after an account is selected to be part of a strategic account program depends on the robust nature of the program itself. If there are specific benefits for the strategic account that have been established as part of the program—that is, greater access to the company's engineering expertise or enhanced customer service when handling the account's orders—these are often articulated in some type of marketing collateral. If this is the case, we suggest that the strategic account manager assigned to the account make a formal presentation to key stakeholders of the account introducing herself or himself as the account manager and explaining the benefits the account will receive by being included in the program. Such a presentation can further enhance the relationship between the two organizations.

Deselection

If a decision is made to deselect a strategic account from the program, extreme caution needs to be followed when deciding on the next steps. The strategic account manager should be close enough to the account to understand the potential reaction should formal communication related to this take place. If the reason for the deselection is because of inactivity by the account or the account's lack of interest in a strategic relationship, it may not be necessary to communicate externally this decision formally because the account has not invested in the program to begin with. If the decision, however, has to do with a lack of revenue or a deterioration in profitability, it may be wise to meet with the account to explain the reason for its removal from the program. In this case, a well-planned presentation by the strategic account leader should be prepared and always include the possibility of reselection should the business relationship change moving forward. Deselection of an account from any strategic account program should be taken very seriously and handled with much sensitivity, significant input, and guidance from the strategic account leader.

As we said at the beginning of this chapter, selection or deselection of strategic accounts is one of the most important activities related to the success of any strategic account program. As important is the selection of strategic account managers or leaders. We cover this in the next chapter.

CHAPTER THREE
Selecting Effective Strategic Account Managers

Strategic Account Management Process

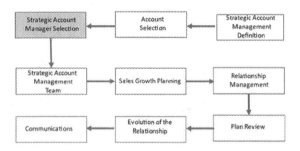

Once the company has selected the accounts that will be part of the strategic account program, it is time to understand the responsibilities of the account managers. And with that comes the selection of the right account managers and determination of the best compensation system with which to incentivize them.

Account Manager Responsibilities

Given that the account management team at times falls structurally within the sales organization, the responsibilities of the strategic account manager need to be understood by the account manager as well as by the rest of the sales organization. This is very important to ensure that all members of the selling organization stay in their "swim lanes."

Following is a list of account manager responsibilities. While they are in principle generic, they may still need to be adjusted to fit the specific account manager role and the overall sales organization's selling philosophy.

- Create a compelling account value proposition and subsequently a strategic account plan.
   o The value proposition gets laid out in the account plan, which needs to provide solutions that meet the needs of the strategic account. This is covered in detail in chapter 5.
- Own the relationship with the strategic account at the corporate level. A good example of this was presented in chapter 1, where the account manager from Dynamic Corporation calling on Acme Corporation, Jill Anderson, owned the relationship with the corporate engineering team.
- Drive the approval and use of all company products and services.
   o Most industrial companies have a formal process of approving suppliers. The account manager is responsible for making sure all the products and/ or services provided by his or her company are approved by the strategic account, so they can be purchased by all strategic account locations.

- Provide assistance with the pursuit of capital projects at the account.
  - o The account leader should be a member of project pursuit teams focused on major capital projects being designed by the leader's strategic account.
- Negotiate strategic contracts on behalf of the company.
  - o As mentioned in chapter 1, global strategic accounts expect to negotiate with a single point person who can speak on behalf of the entire company.
- Mitigate risk for the account should issues arise.
  - o We saw this as well in chapter 1, where the account manager needed to assist Acme Corporation with delivery issues taking place at its China locations.
- Leverage resources with the company to mitigate risk and drive specific programs for the account.
  - o Again, as we discussed in chapter 1, the strategic account effort needs to be an enterprise-wide effort. The strategic account manager needs to leverage resources from within the company to mitigate risk and drive account specific programs forward.
- Create and execute a communication plan and rhythm both internally with the support team and externally with the account.
  - o We discuss this in more detail in chapter 9.
- Follow the operating rhythm established by the overall strategic account program leader on a weekly, monthly, quarterly, and annual basis. Note we have included a suggested operating rhythm in the appendix.

Hiring Decisions

There are several questions that need to be addressed when deciding on how to choose account leaders for your strategic account effort.

- Do you hire from within your organization or go outside?
- If you hire from inside your organization, in which departments do you look?
- Should you focus on candidates with longer tenure and more experience, or should this role be looked at as a next step in the career of a high-potential employee?
- What are the qualifications and skills needed to be a successful strategic account manager?

We now explore each of these questions.

From Inside or Outside Your Organization?

Whether you hire an account manager from within your organization or outside of it will depend very much on the account itself.

In general, we believe there are great benefits to hiring account managers from within your own organization. First, they already have a good understanding of the industry in which you operate. Second, they may have some knowledge of the interaction with the strategic account simply from being a part of the organization. Third and most important, as a part of your organization, they hopefully have a sound reputation within the company, understand how to get things done within the organization, and can therefore bring value quickly to the strategic account.

With that being said, should it be determined that a given strategic account is extraordinarily complex and/or that the knowledge of the account itself and understanding its culture and people are very critical to success, it might make sense to look outside the company. In this case, it might be best to recruit a strategic account manager from a similar industry who is currently or was at one time the strategic account manager for that account. If this is the path that is followed, it is particularly important to find out how the strategic account perceives that current or past account manager. It is also important to understand that the account leader will enter the company without an existing reputation and understanding of the company culture or mechanics. In short, while the outside candidate may not have a learning curve related to the customer, the candidate could have a significant learning curve related to the company itself.

So in general, we feel that hiring from within is preferred for the reasons we mentioned unless knowledge about the account or relationships within the account are deemed to be most important.

From Which Departments?

This question may seem to be easily answered; of course, you would promote from within the sales department. Not necessarily. While sales might be the right place to look when selecting an account leader, the account may have needs that suggest looking elsewhere. For example, if you are dealing with an account that has multiple facilities located around the world and a need for your products or services at each one, that account might best be supported by a candidate who comes from the manufacturing or operations part of the organization. That person might be able to leverage specific knowledge to bring impactful value to the strategic account. Likewise, if a strategic account values cocreation of solutions that address the account's needs, it might make sense to look for a candidate in the engineering or technical department within the company.

Of course, it is not unusual for sales representatives to be excellent candidates for strategic account managers. They usually have the negotiation and personal skills that help the account be successful. However, our recommendation is to keep an open mind, and focus on the specific needs of the account. It may be possible to find the best candidate outside the sales organization.

Experience or Potential?

Another question that needs to be addressed when searching for account manager candidates is whether you hire someone with significant experience (where this could be the final position in a long career) or someone with limited experience and use the account manager position as a stepping-stone in a promising career. Like the decision to hire from inside or outside the company, this often depends on the customer for which the account manager will be responsible.

It is common for key contacts in some accounts to expect that they will be serviced by an account leader with significant experience in their industry and deep knowledge of the products or services they use. In this case, it may be wise to hire or promote someone with an abundance of experience. Some accounts, however, may have a more progressive attitude and respond better to someone earlier in her or his career. They may also have a long-term prospective and see the benefits a less-experienced yet energetic candidate may be able to provide the account as the manager rises through the company.

The decision to hire a more-experienced or less-experienced individual may also be part of a corporate human resources strategy. As we indicated earlier, the company may decide to use the account manager position to provide experience to high-potential candidates as they prove themselves in their careers. As a result, a company may have a mix of account managers who are in the final stages of their careers, where the account leader job will be the last before they retire, as well as employees who use this position to gain valuable experience as they move up in the company. We believe this is a sound strategy as it provides the less-experienced employees with valuable interaction with longer-term strategic account team members from whom they can certainly learn much.

What Qualifications and Skills Are Needed?

As discussed previously, account managers may come from various departments within a company and have varying levels of experience. Still, in many cases when a company searches for an account manager, a job description must be created. That job description typically lists qualifications necessary to be considered for the job as well as skills that will be helpful once in the job. These need to be tailored to the specific account management position, but they could include:

Qualifications

- A minimum four-year college degree, depending on the type of company. This could be more restrictive; for example, require a degree in engineering.

- At least seven years of sales or account management experience. As mentioned earlier, many account leaders do have sales backgrounds
- Experience developing and implementing strategic plans
- Demonstrate strong business acumen
- Demonstrate strong drive for results
- Be a self-starter and have the ability to work in an ambiguous environment
- Experience using multiple information technology tools

Skills

- A customer focus
- Presentation skills
- Communication skills
- Interpersonal savvy
- Political savvy
- Ability to motivate others
- Ability to influence others without direct authority
- Good listening skills
- Ability to create and understand business financials
- Good and effective negotiating skills
- Prioritizing, planning, and organizing skills

These are good examples of general qualifications and skills for the account manager. However, one qualification that we believe is absolutely critical in a strategic account manager is to demonstrate strong business acumen. Even if you select a person earlier in his or her career, the potential manager should be demonstrating this quality. In general, employees of a targeted account want to deal with a well-rounded individual who understands business overall, not just a specific part of it. People with this qualification are able to deliver more quality to the strategic account. We include a sample job description in the appendix referencing many of these competencies and traits. This can be used as a template for creating a complete job description.

Strategic Account Manager Compensation

The compensation package for a strategic account manager varies depending on his or her background. If, as discussed earlier, the individual is a seasoned professional who has held significant leadership positions within the company, compensation will need to reflect the experience that individual brings to the new position. In fact, it is not uncommon for seasoned strategic account managers to have a salary equal to high-level executives within the same company. If the strategic account manager is a high-potential employee and the position is being used as a stepping-stone to higher-level positions within the company, the manager's salary will be reflective of another upward move in a promising career.

Incentive plans for strategic account managers vary greatly depending on the sophistication of the overall strategic account program. We believe the most relevant metric to be used in a strategic account incentive plan is share of wallet; that is, the percentage of business the company receives of the total spend by the strategic account. An increase in share of wallet demonstrates that the account strategy/plan is being executed effectively by the account manager and the entire team. The difficulty in determining share of wallet is that significant input by the strategic account is required.

If share of wallet is not obtainable, we suggest the next best metrics would be account order intake and profitability. These should be weighed equally. Clearly, a company would not want to see revenue growth at the expense of profitability or vice versa. These two metrics require significant support from IT and/or finance as this information needs to be gathered from all account locations globally, which could be a significant challenge.

When companies have disparate ERP systems, reporting global order intake and profitability by strategic account can be very difficult if not impossible. If that is the case, we suggest using higher-level metrics such as business unit revenue, business unit bookings, business operating income, or a combination of all three. While this is not directly tied to the performance of the strategic account manager, one would hope that if business unit revenue, bookings, or operating income targets are achieved, some of that was the result of positive performance by the company's most important customers.

Please note that these incentive metrics should also be a part of the compensation of the virtual strategic account team members, which we discuss in the next chapter.

With the account manager in place, understanding the manager's responsibilities, and having established a compensation/incentive plan, the company needs to decide how it will structure the team that will work with the manager to deliver value to the account. We address this topic in the next chapter.

CHAPTER FOUR
The Strategic Account Management Team

Strategic Account Management Process

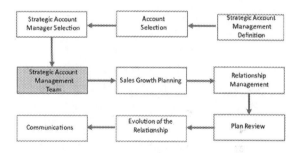

The last chapter focused on the selection of the strategic account manager. Once the strategic account manager is in place, it is time to put together a team so that the account plan can be effectively executed. A strategic account manager can bring significant value to an account, however, he or she cannot leverage the company's resources to deliver that value unless there is a team built from various parts of the company to help.

Similarly to the selection of accounts into the program,

there is no single way to develop a strategic account team. Generally, the more people who are on the team and the more disciplines that are represented, the more successful the effort will be. An effective strategic account team could include the following disciplines or individuals:

- Executive sponsor
- Strategic account manager
- Account program manager
- Sales site team leaders
- Finance
- Manufacturing/operations
- Marketing
- Customer service
- Engineering/product management

Most of these team members will be part of a virtual team. That is, they do not report directly to the strategic account manager but to their respective disciplines. However, it is imperative that they be engaged and willing to be a contributing member of the team. They need to understand and effectively fulfill their roles on the team. Following is a brief description of the input provided by each discipline on the team.

Executive Sponsor

This position provides high-level engagement with the strategic account, eliminates barriers within the company that can provide value to the account, and mitigates risk that can jeopardize the relationship with the account. Please refer to the executive sponsor description in the "Relationship Management" section in chapter five for more details.

Strategic Account Manager

These responsibilities are covered in chapter 3.

Account Program Manager

This role requires a more detailed explanation. As a strategic account program grows and matures, it may be helpful to add a program manager role. Program managers provide critical support to the strategic account manager. In most cases, they support several strategic account managers. If the program manager handles only one account, the manager will most likely report directly to the strategic account manager. If the program manager handles several accounts, reporting would typically be to the director or leader of the entire strategic account program. Typical responsibilities for a program manager are to:

- Provide assistance with the development of the strategic account plan
- Lead the development of contracts with the strategic account
- Assist with any information requests from the strategic account
- Assist marketing with collateral to promote the account's value proposition
- Provide data collection and analysis needed by the strategic account manager
- Assist the strategic account manager with risk mitigation when needed
- Meet with the strategic account when requested by the account leader

This role is not a part of every strategic program, but it definitely adds to the effectiveness of the strategic account manager and the overall positive impact on the strategic account. In short, the program manager supports the strategic account manager and allows him or her to spend more time working directly with the strategic account personnel, which is where they can be most effective. While strategic account managers can come from inside or outside the organization and can be early in their careers or later, we have found that the most successful program managers have spent time as project managers/engineers within the company. We include a sample job description for a strategic account program manager in the appendix.

Sales Site Team Leaders

These are the individuals who call on the critical strategic account locations. They play key roles in making certain that the strategic account plan is effectively executed. They need to make sure that the initiatives established in the account plan are rolled out at their respective locations. They also need to provide feedback to the strategic account manager on how these initiatives are being received at their locations. It is especially important for a site team leader to make the strategic account manager aware of any issues that require risk mitigation or ones that will have negative impacts on the relationship with the account as a whole.

Finance

Each strategic account team needs a representative from finance who can provide regular updates on financial issues related to the account. Monthly sales and profit information is critical, as well as any credit/accounts receivable issues.

Manufacturing/Operations

This representative typically provides information on the company's on-time delivery statistics with the account by location. This can be used to mitigate risk if the information is not positive or promote the company and the relationship should it be positive. This person also leads initiatives within the account plan that are focused on providing products or services to a specific strategic account location or new products that are the result of a cocreated solution.

Marketing

Marketing often provides collateral specific to the account that can enhance the relationship. This could be in the form of brochures that can provide details on products or services available to the account or in the form of a survey that can provide important feedback on the performance of the company's products, services, or customer service.

Customer Service

If there is a customer service initiative as part of the strategic plan, this representative would be responsible for making sure this part of the plan is executed. Likewise, should there be any favorable or unfavorable information related to customer service, this representative would be expected to report on this. In addition, most strategic accounts require that key performance indicators (KPIs) be tracked and reported regularly. These could include metrics on things such as on time delivery of orders, quality issues, order-entry mistakes, and time from order receipt to order entry. Even though the data for these metrics may come from other departments, the responsibility for gathering and reporting this information is often assigned to customer service. This is especially common when there is no program manager assigned to the strategic account to handle this responsibility.

Engineering/Product Management

Should specific product development or enhancements be part of the strategic account plan, this person would be responsible for the execution of this project. Also, should any product-quality issues develop, it would be the responsibility of this person to investigate and address this situation.

As we said earlier, most of the team members are virtual team members who report directly to their disciplines. The area where this frequently varies is with the site team leaders. They can report directly to the sales regions where they reside, or they can handle several strategic account locations within a region and report directly to the strategic account manager. Both options are shown in the following organization charts. Also, note that in both organization charts, the program manager(s) report to the overall strategic account program director. It is possible that the program managers could report directly to the strategic account managers. This would be most common when a program manager supports only one strategic account.

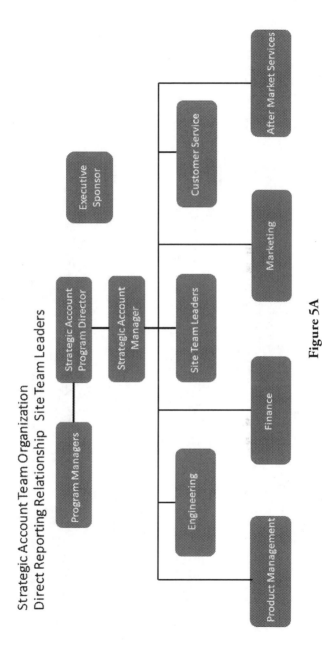

Strategic Account Team Organization
Direct Reporting Relationship   Site Team Leaders

Figure 5A

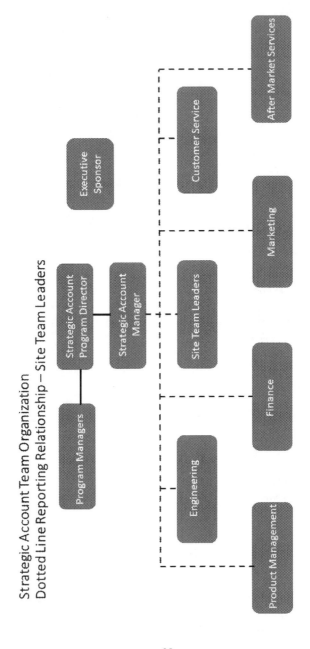

Figure 5B

Team Rhythm

In chapter 7 we discuss the frequency and content of both internal and external review meetings. Suffice it to say that it is especially important to settle on a regular and consistent team rhythm. At a minimum, we believe the entire account team needs to meet once a quarter to review the account financials and discuss the overall progress related to the strategic account plan. As the year nears the end, the team must meet frequently to develop the account plan for the following year. The number of meetings required for this is really determined by the strategic account leader. Regardless, the key is to have the full cooperation and participation of every member of the team.

CHAPTER FIVE

The Strategic Account Sales Growth Planning Process

Strategic Account Management Process

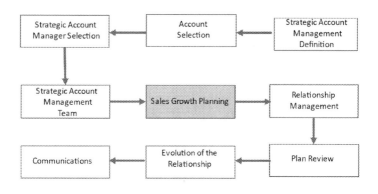

Once the strategic account program is properly sized, the account selections completed, the organizational alignment and commitments attained, and the account managers assigned, we can start the planning process. The planning work should be led by the assigned strategic account manager to force the manager to become intimate with the customer.

This level of intimacy increases the chances of creating a highly effective plan that can be executed successfully.

Situational Analysis

First things first. In order to identify the best opportunities for growth and subsequently create the sales plan, we need to gain a full understanding of the situation with the account. We call this first step the *situational analysis*. The situational analysis should paint a clear picture of the customer's business concerns and strategies, the competitive landscape, and our position and relevance to the strategic account. It is through this robust review of the situation that we will be able to identify where and how we can add value to our customer's objectives.

Strategic Account Business Analysis

Let's start with the customer. To better serve the target account, we need to understand on a detailed level the account's mission, vision, financial health, concerns, and short-term as well as long-term plans. In short, we need to go through a deep dive of the account's business from A to Z. A perfect place to start is the annual report if one is published. The annual report provides a wealth of information crucial to the account manager's analysis, starting with a detailed description of the type of business with which it is engaged, the products and services it provides, the industry segment it serves, the leadership position it views itself as having, and most important, the company's vision of its future.

Once the strategic account manager gains an understanding of the target customer's business, the manager can research the company's industry segment to identify its trends, its competitors' positions in the market, and the key metrics used to gauge the level of success each player enjoys.

The annual report will also have information regarding the target customer's financial strength. We recommend carefully reviewing at least three consecutive reports to obtain the results for the last several years. The intent here is to determine the company's growth trends and then use this information to compare it with the results of its peers.

If the target account does not publish an annual report, the required information will need to be obtained through other means. The most reliable way to gather this information is through conversations with key strategic account individuals willing to share financial results, strategic imperatives, and concerns that keep company executives awake at night. In today's world, the research work is facilitated by the internet and search engines available therein. Several sources may provide insight on privately owned companies. The following sites may be helpful:

- dnb.com
- gopher.com
- index.about.com
- simpli.com

In addition to traditional financial metrics such as revenue, gross margin, and operating income, the strategic account manager should identify and keep track of KPIs pertinent to the strategic account business and industry segment. The following are typical examples for consideration:

- Annual capital expenditures
- Barrel of oil equivalent replacement ratios (for the oil and gas industry)
- Research and development expense per new drug developed (for the pharmaceutical industry)
- TAKT times (time elapsed between two-unit completions in order to meet demand) applied to manufacturing enterprises

Furthermore, it is worth keeping track of specific KPIs that are of concern to the strategic account's management team. These may include safety, quality, productivity KPIs, and so on.

As we progress with the strategic account's business analysis, we need to create organizational matrices. These matrices should describe the different levels of the target account's organization, for example,

- Board of directors
- Leadership team
- Management team
- Procurement and sourcing function
- Other specific functions involved in the procurement decision-making of the products and services you provide. For example,
  - Engineering
  - Accounting
  - IT

A great way to present this information is by arranging it in an organizational chart format. Figure 6 is an example of a supply chain organizational chart for reference.

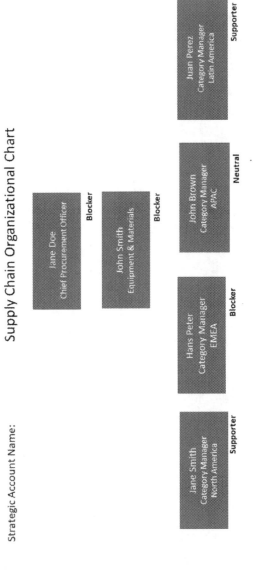

Strategic Account Name:

Supply Chain Organizational Chart

Figure 6

This information will become useful during the creation of the relationship management plan, which is covered later. Note that each person listed has been assigned an attitude or disposition related to the company.

Another tool you will need to develop as part of the customer business analysis is a list of their critical sites. These locations are the actual users of the products and services you provide. The list is a tool that is used for several tasks including, but not limited to, the following:

- Virtual team member assignment
- Installed base estimation by site
- Relationship status with site's management team

We find it of great value to match the assigned virtual team member to each strategic account critical site. We recommend this be done by use of the account manager's team matrix. Please refer to the sample template shown in figure 7 as a guide for the creation of a critical site list.

Critical Site List						
Customer	Virtual Team Member Assigned to Site	Relationship Status with Site's Management	Installed Base			
Critical Site Name			Product 1	Product 2	Product 3	Product 4

Figure 7

A crucial part of the customer business analysis is the identification of key initiatives and concerns. By understanding its initiatives, we can then look to find enablers within our basket of products and services that can facilitate the strategic account's achievement of its goals. Concurrently, by having knowledge of what keeps the account's management team awake at night, we can find solutions within our toolbox to dissipate these concerns and bring peace of mind to its executive team.

Once the initiatives and concerns are identified, the strategic account manager may create a table matching the strategic account's initiatives and concerns with the company's products or services that would enable the achievement of the objectives and/or dissipate strategic account management's concerns. Figure 8 is an example of a customer strategies and enabling solutions matrix, which allows the strategic account team to identify customer strategies and initiatives and then match those with offerings by the strategic account that can potentially address those.

Customer Strategies and Enabling Solutions				
Customer: Acme	**Customer Strategies**			
Customer Initiatives	**Strategy 1 Leverage supply chain.**	**Strategy 2 Source more-effective specialty widgets.**	**Strategy 3**	**Strategy 4**
Initiative 1	Develop global enterprise frame agreements.	Reduce specialty widget service by 25%.		
Initiative 2	Focus on global manufacturers.	Reduce widget power consumption.		
Initiative 3	Partner with those providing global aftermarket service capability.	Improve on-time delivery of specialty widgets.		
Company Enablers	**Company Solutions**	**Company Solutions**	**Company Solutions**	**Company Solutions**
Solution 1	Strategic account manager negotiates globally.	Leverage product development to design new specialty widget.		
Solution 2	Complete construction of plant in South America.	Design low-power widgets.		
Solution 3	Create service facilities in Asia to complete global service footprint.	Complete lean projects in all manufacturing locations to reduce lead times and improve on-time delivery.		

Figure 8

The business portion of the situational analysis is almost complete. All the information gathered so far allows the account manager to identify strengths, weaknesses, opportunities, and threats that lead to a SWOT analysis of the target account. The SWOT will be a useful tool when we develop our sales growth plan. To be clear, these are the strengths, opportunities, weaknesses, and threats from the perspective of the strategic account.

A sample SWOT template is shown in figure 9.

SWOT ANALYSIS

For Strategic Account ▓
For Company ☐

Strengths	Weaknesses
• Industry Leadership • Financial strength • Global Footprint	• Organizational rigidity • CAPEX Projections • Market Outlook
Opportunities	**Threats**
• Project A • Need for customized widgets • Leverage Supply Chain	• Political Instability • Potential CAPEX Reductions • Divestitures

Key insights:
Seek global enterprise frame agreement

Figure 9

Competitive Landscape and Analysis

Since we have completed our deep dive into the strategic account's business, we now analyze the competitive landscape. This evaluation requires that we interact with our customer as we need input to determine which competitors are relevant to their business.

There are several aspects of the evaluation that require the target account's input:

- Product and/or service groups
- Top competitors
- Critical procurement decision factors
- Weighting of each procurement decision factor
- Scoring for the company and its main competitors by product and/or service group

Product and/or Service Groups. As we look at our product portfolio, we need to determine which groups are pertinent to the account's business. This determination should be based on a twofold process:

a. Check annual revenue by product for a minimum of three years.
b. Interview key players within the customer's organization.

Top Competitors. Although you feel you have a good idea as to who your main competitors are, we urge you to interview key strategic account individuals involved in the procurement decision-making of the products and services you offer.

Critical Procurement Decision Factors. Pardon the redundancy, but this is a critical part of the competitive analysis. It is extremely important that the most pertinent buying criteria are selected. There is no other way to guarantee this than to interview your customers for their input. We recommend you organize these factors into three categories as follows:

- Product- and/or services-related factors. The following are some examples for consideration:
  - o Quality-related factors
  - o Price
  - o Delivery
  - o Product fitness for application
- Company-related factors. A few examples are listed below:
  - o Ease of doing business
  - o Global footprint
  - o Engineering and/or application support
  - o Innovation capacity
  - o Aftermarket support
- Sales team–related factors
  - o Technical knowledge
  - o Availability to the customer
  - o Responsiveness

Weighting of Each Critical Procurement Decision Factor. How important is each buying decision factor to the customer? Only the strategic account can answer this question. We recommend that once you have established the key factors your customer has determined relevant to its business that you ask them to rate each in importance using a 1–5 scale, 1 being least important, and 5 being extremely important.

Scoring. As you may be able to tell, we now have most of the ingredients to create the competitor rating tool. A sample tool is shown in figure 10.

Competitive Matrix

Product Group:	Customer: Acme			Scores							
				Dynamic Corporation		Globex		Competitor 2		Competitor 3	
Rating related to	Buying decision factor importance	Weighting		Score	Weighted Score	Score	Weighted Score	Score	Weighted Score	Score	Weighted Score
Product	Quality	5		5	25	4	20	3	15		
	Price	4		2	8	4	16	5	20		
	Delivery	3		4	12	2	6	4	12		
	Fit for purpose	2		5	10	3	6	2	4		
Company	Ease of doing business	5		3	15	3	15	3	15		
	Global footprint	4		5	20	4	16	3	12		
	Aftermarket support	3		4	12	3	9	3	9		
	Innovation capability	2		3	6	2	4	1	2		
Salesteam	Technical knowledge	5		5	25	4	20	2	10		
	Availability	4		4	16	4	16	5	20		
	Responsiveness	3		4	12	3	9	4	12		
Totals					161		137		131		

Figure 10

Once you confirmed with your account the competitors to be evaluated, along with the buying decision factors including their score weighting, all that is left is for your customer to rate each procurement decision factor for each supplier. Again, we recommend you use a 1–5 scale, 1 depicting a poor score, and 5 being an excellent or highest score. The competitive matrix should become a reference tool that will assist with the creation of our sales strategic plan and, more specifically, with our offensive and defensive initiatives.

We recommend that each virtual team member produce a competitive matrix for the critical site for which they are responsible. This exercise will assist the team member with the creation and execution of initiatives that may be specific to the site.

Company Position within the Strategic Account

The final step in our situational analysis involves the review of our position within the target account. To begin, we need to evaluate the financial picture including, but not limited to, the following metrics for each product and/or service group, preferably over a four-year period:

- Revenue
- Gross margin
- Operating income
- Revenue to sales expense ratio
- Revenue compounded annual growth rate (CAGR) over the four-year period

The intent is to determine our revenue and profitability growth rate trends as well as our cost to serve the account. Our expectation is to maintain growth rates above the company's average.

As discussed earlier in the book, a crucial strategic account related KPI is termed "share of wallet." This metric is attained by calculating the ratio between the company's annual revenue for each product or service group supplied and the customer's total annual spend for each product and/or service group.

Annual Product Group Revenue: Customer Annual Spend

This metric provides an accurate picture of the company's penetration levels within the target account. It is the responsibility of the strategic account manager to identify the customer's annual spend figures as without a valid estimation of the strategic account's total investment in the product or service in question, the share of wallet accuracy is diminished. Since this KPI measures our level of penetration with the account, and since customer annual spends may vary from year to year, we recommend you update this metric on an annual basis.

Our position with the account should include a SWOT analysis that is specific to our relationship with the customer. We would use the same SWOT template as shown in figure 9. Once we have completed the SWOT, we should derive our key findings and insights. Unlike the strategic account SWOT, this SWOT indicates *our* strengths and weaknesses and *our* opportunities and threats with the target account.

There are two additional tools we recommend using as part of the evaluation of our position with the target account. These are:

- Product portfolio status
- Offering potential matrix

Product Portfolio Status. This tool assists the account manager with the positioning of each product and/or service group with the account. The results attained allow for the identification of activities to either shore up a product's preferred position or for the creation of strategies to improve less than preferred status with the strategic account. A sample template is depicted in figure 11.

Product Portfolio Status			
Customer: Acme	**Status**		
Product/Service	**None**	**Acceptable**	**Preferred**
Fashionable widgets		X	
High-performance widgets			X
Engineered widgets			X
Widget service		X	
Key Insights: High performance and engineered widgets have a preferred status and are heavily relied on by Acme.			

Figure 11

Offering Potential Matrix. The matrix shown in figure 12 is a powerful tool that intends to match the company's product and service offerings with the customer's initiatives, strategies, and concerns.

Offering Potential Matrix						
Customer: Acme	High-Performance Widgets		Engineered Widgets		Reduce Service	
Customer Initiatives/ Concerns	Rating	Comments	Rating	Comments	Rating	Comments
Reduce widget service by 25%	3	Launch initiatives to defend our installed base	1	Promote our engineered/ low maintenance widgets	2	Expand widget monitoring services to drive maintenance cost reductions
Reduce widget power consumption	2	Promote our low power widget portfolio	1	Drive low power engineered product development	1	Drive widget monitoring services to measure power consumption reduction
Partner with those providing global aftermarket service capability	N/A		N/A		2	Expand aftermarket service footprint

Rating Scale:

1—Low potential

2—Moderate potential

3—High potential

Figure 12

On completion of the customer position analysis, the strategic account manager should be able to answer the following question: How important is the company to the strategic account?

In summary, the tools completed during the situational analysis—including the Site Locations Matrix, the Customer Strategies and Enabling Solutions Matrix, the SWOT Analysis for both the customer and the company, the Competitive Matrix, the Product Portfolio Status, and the Offering Potential Matrix—will become the pillars for the strategic account manager's formulation of the objectives, initiatives, and strategies both on the defensive as well as the offensive sides of the field.

Sales Growth Plan

Now that we have the situational analysis completed, we can start with the creation of our sales plan as the sales growth plan will be constructed using the information obtained from the situational analysis. The first step of the growth plan process involves the identification of the opportunities. These opportunities need to be evaluated, sorted, and prioritized. Then specific initiatives need to be developed for each opportunity. Each initiative needs to have a team member assigned and a timeline established for completion.

The account manager should segregate opportunities by category. Several categories may be pertinent depending on the industry segment served. In all cases, however, the strategic account manager will uncover activities required to defend the company's position with the target account and other potential initiatives to attack any competitor's installed base. Furthermore, the situational analysis should make evident opportunities for growth with the account leading to an increase of its share of wallet. For example, in the manufacturing sector, these opportunities may be segmented in capital project–based and aftermarket opportunities.

Defensive Initiatives

The company SWOT and the competitive analysis should be the first areas the strategic account manager reviews for the identification of any moves the company needs to take to defend its current position with the target account. Once clarity is obtained, the account manager must work with the virtual team to determine initiatives by critical site that need to be put in place to protect the company's current business. In the manufacturing sector, these may range from the proper sizing of our inventory at hand for fast response to customer replacement needs to the formation of cradle-to-grave aftermarket asset management organizations to manage customer's equipment, parts warehouses, maintenance, repair, and operation activities.

Again, these defensive activities need to be specific to each customer location. Thus, it becomes imperative that each virtual team member takes on the responsibility to formulate a plan, gain the necessary resources, and execute the agreed-on initiatives within the committed timelines.

Offensive Initiatives

The situational analysis should have uncovered numerous areas that can be turned into offensive-based opportunities. Look for competitors' weaknesses on which you may be able to capitalize. Any opportunity to convert their current businesses should be identified and pursued. The search for offensive opportunities should also be brought to the critical site level as most competitors' weaknesses that warrant offensive measures are not normally applicable to all customer locations.

Capital Projects

Once defensive and offensive initiatives are developed, the strategic account manager should start looking at the target account's near, mid, and long-term growth plans. These may include plant revamps (brownfield projects), new construction (greenfield projects), and/or environmental, health and safety investments. Furthermore, should your products and services contribute to the digitization, modernization, and remote control of plant infrastructure, it becomes incumbent on the account manager to identify specific opportunities with the strategic account. This is especially true if the company enjoys a planning partner or trusted-adviser status with the customer (see chapter 6 for status details).

As our relationship status rises with the strategic account, the account manager should seek ways to become aware of their project investments early during the feasibility stages. We need to become part of the planning process and assist project designers customer engineering teams and contracted external design engineering firms with proposals for our technology/product/services selections that provide maximum value in terms of cost of ownership, efficient performance, and optimal fit for purpose applications. Sales funnel tools should be designed in a manner that encourages early engagement. Here, there are numerous customer relationship management tools commercially available for use.

Once opportunities are identified, they need to be sized, prioritized, and tracked. We suggest using the tool shown in figure 13 to collect the estimated revenue increases forecasted for each initiative.

Strategic Initiatives Revenue Contribution					
Strategic Opportunity	Tasks	Year 1	Year 2	Year 3	3 Year Total
Initiative 1	ABC				
Initiative 2	DEF				
Initiative 3	GHI				
Initiative 4	JKL				
Initiative 5	MNO				
Initiative 6	PQR				
Total Estimated Incremental Growth					

Figure 13

Figure 14 provides an overall view of the growth impact to the business, including the base business, estimated market growth impact, and the contribution attained through the initiatives depicted above.

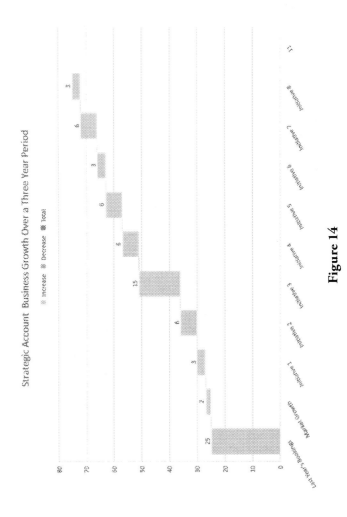

Strategic Account Business Growth Over a Three Year Period

Figure 14

CHAPTER SIX
The Relationship Management Plan

Strategic Account Management Process

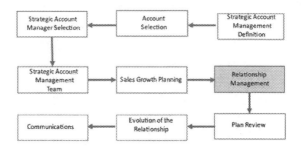

Strategic plans may be well designed with realizable objectives that drive growth and profitability. However, no plan will succeed without proper execution. In order to ensure strategic account managers have a successful execution strategy, they must identify and maintain strong relationships with the account's key individuals involved in the product/service selection and procurement process. This requirement is not exclusive to the account manager but also to all virtual team members with their critical site relationships.

Assessment and Planning

Relationships in business, as in life, are complex. Many facets need to be addressed for them to blossom and last. One may develop relationships with the right people, and then again, relationships may develop with individuals who are unable to add value to your goals.

Therefore, the strategic account manager needs to first and foremost identify the right people within the strategic account organization they will target to develop relationships. The operative words in the above sentence are "right people." We should not only concentrate on the C-level individuals or the procurement team members, but on all individuals in the organization who may influence the buying decision-making process. They may belong to the technical, engineering, operations, or financial function but have a role in procurement-selection activities.

Once all the individuals and their roles are identified, we need to proceed with the assessment for each key player. This assessment requires that several aspects of the relationship be evaluated, starting with their specific roles in the procurement decision-making process. The person being assessed may have different roles as shown in figure 15.

The account manager will also want to identify each key individual's attitude or disposition toward the company she or he represents. Note that the individual may appreciate the value our products and services bring to the strategic account but may have a neutral position in or may be a detractor of the procurement of the company's offerings. Please refer to figure 15 for details.

Successful and long-lasting business relationships develop over time and require that the strategic account manager address at a minimum the following account targeted individual's needs and wants:

- Individual's immediate personal and professional needs and obligations
- Individual's medium- and long-term goals
- Individual's growth plans within the strategic account organization

When evaluating the account key individual's professional needs, it becomes imperative that the account manager learn how said person is measured and rewarded. By understanding what will make the individual successful within the strategic account organization, the account manager may be able to align the company's offerings and solutions to match the person's needs, and as a consequence, demonstrate value in a manner that not only impacts the organization but also the employee's professional growth.

In a nutshell, we need to identify the key person's "hot buttons" we are to push to advance our objectives.

The strategic account manager should also decide who within the team may be better aligned to develop and manage the relationship with each of the account's key contacts. The account manager, with the collaboration of all pertinent team members, must determine what actions and activities are to take place to grow the relationship with each key contact. The chances of successful execution of the strategic plan increase as the relationship developed with the account's key players gains greater depth.

There are several ways to manage these relationships. We suggest you utilize the Relationship Assessment and Management Plan tool (figure 15.) to collect all the information and activities on one page.

Relationship Assessment and Management Plan							
Customer: Acme							
Individual Name	Title and Role	Buying Decision Responsibility	Attitude toward Company	Individual Professional Drivers/Needs	Individual Personal Drivers/Needs	Who in Our Team Is Aligned with This Individual?	Actions to Grow Relationship
Jane Wilson	Procurement	Approver	Neutral	Cost reduction	Recognition with superiors	SAM	Global agreement
Russ Johnson	Technical	Influencer	Advocate	Fit for purpose	Promotion	S Adams	Improve portfolio
Juan Gomez	Engineering	Recommender	Supporter	Quality	No issues	SAM	Promote product 2
Title and Role Scale	**Buying Decision Responsibility Scale**	**Attitude w/ Company Scale**					
Finance	Approver	Advocate					
Procurement	Decision maker	Supporter					
Technical	Recommender	Neutral					
Operations	Influencer	Blocker					
Engineering	Other						
Other							

Figure 15

Finally, the strategic account manager and team will have to rate the overall relationship status between the company and the strategic account. This KPI is an extremely important, though normally subjective metric intended to rate the depth of the overall company status with the customer. Based on the status level attained, the strategic account manager along with management may find it necessary to assign an executive sponsor. A sample relationship status scale is shown in figure 16.

Company Relationship Status Scale	
Trusted Adviser	☐
Planning Partner	☐
Preferred Vendor	☐
Vendor	☐

Figure 16

The scale shown in figure 16 is our recommended way of segmenting the company's customer base. As you can tell, the scale depicts four status levels that can defined as follows:

a. *Vendor:* This is the lowest status level normally assigned to customers who will consider the company's products and services equal to all other competitors but is unable to discern additional value by dealing with your firm. Thus, the customer normally makes procurement decisions based on either price or delivery.

b. *Preferred Vendor:* At this level, the customer views the company's offerings of greater value compared to other competitors. This level is generally attained with offerings that may have superior performances compared to some other competitors, or it may be due to improved customer service, product availability, or cost.

c. *Planning Partner:* As the relationship evolves, the company must continue to develop differentiating value for the strategic account and seek to become inserted in the customer's procurement-planning process. The advantage of reaching planning-partner status includes a firsthand look at opportunities, a better understanding of customer expectations, and consequently, an improved position to secure a greater percentage of the strategic account's share of wallet.

d. *Trusted Adviser:* This is the highest relationship status level. When reaching this level, the strategic account views your organization as an adviser to their procurement strategies for the products and services you offer. Your organization will be best situated to seek partnering opportunities, attain exclusive rights to the target account's business, and in short, drive superior sales growth rates compared to the firm's business with customers situated at lower relationship status levels.

In conclusion, one key organizational objective in your strategic account plan is to drive the firm's relationship status positioning at a minimum one level up within agreed-on timelines with management.

Executive Sponsorship

As your company makes progress with the sales plan, becomes more relevant to the customer, and consequently moves up the relationship status scale, it may be time to appoint an executive sponsor to the account. There are several reasons to appoint a high-level company executive to a strategic account. The strategic account must feel that your company is becoming an integral part of its operation and thus, have a desire to deal in a more intimate manner with your firm. It is an opportunity to move to a planning-partner or trusted-adviser status. It opens the door for earlier knowledge of the strategic account's strategies, initiatives, concerns, and plans. It provides an enhanced overall customer experience to the strategic account. It allows for accelerated product portfolio expansion with the customer. In short, it provides an opportunity to carve out a larger share of wallet through collaboration.

Assuming your firm has reached at least a preferred vendor status with the target account, it is the strategic account manager's task to determine the customer's desire or willingness to increase face time at the executive level. Thus, consultations with the strategic account's technical, procurement, operations, and if possible, executive levels are required.

During the review with the target account, one must evaluate the current position of all product and service offerings, if possible, by critical site. The review should identify those offerings that are currently popular with the account as well as those with potential but have currently not found a significant position within the customer's operations. We recommend reviewing figure 12 with the strategic account key individuals as part of this process.

If both parties conclude that an executive sponsorship program will add value to both firms, the next step is to identify the executives who can commit to the relationship. It would be ideal if the strategic account nominated its candidate prior to selecting a company executive. This would allow an opportunity to seek the right match. We propose using the selection and pairing tool shown in figure 17 to facilitate the process.

Executive Sponsor Selection and Pairing Tool		
Traits	**Potential Strategic Account Executive Name:**	**Potential Company Executive Name:**
Education	Texas A&M Master Engineering	Colorado University Mechanical Engineering
Languages	English	English, Spanish
Work History	30 years in strategic accounts organization	20 years in strategic account organization
Product Knowledge	Medium	High
Industry Knowledge	High	High
Personality	Type A	Type B
Hobbies	Fishing, wine collector	Fishing, reading
Sports	Football	Football
Availability	Flexible	Tight schedule

Figure 17

At the end of the day, it becomes evident that by selecting an executive who can develop the right chemistry with their strategic account counterpart, the company will be able to strengthen the relationship at a much faster pace.

Executive sponsorship programs require clear definitions

of the roles and responsibilities of the strategic account manager and executive sponsor. The actual roles may vary depending on the firm's organizational structure, but generally speaking, it is the account manager's responsibility to manage the account, including issue resolution matters. The executive sponsor should look to be a mentoring force to the strategic account manager. Further, the executive sponsor should be the strategic account's voice with the firm's leadership team, should open the doors to further collaboration, and in summary, should have a role in driving the relationship to trusted-adviser status. We propose the list of responsibilities shown in figure 18 for reference.

Strategic Account Manager Versus Executive Sponsor Responsibilities

Strategic Account Manager Responsibilities	Executive Sponsor Responsibilities
○ SAM explains the program to the SA executive • SAM obtains SA agreement to move forward with the program • SAM identifies key executives within SA interested in becoming engaged ○ SAM pairs Company executive sponsor with the SA ○ SAM reviews SA account plan with the executive sponsor ○ SAM remains single point of contact (SPOC) for the account ○ Provides periodic SA plan update to ES ○ Holds annual performance review meeting with SA	○ Commits to being an engaged and reliable executive sponsor ○ Becomes the SA advocate within the company's Leadership Team ○ Commits to attend annual performance review meetings ○ Mentors and guides SAM ○ Is open and responsive to major issue resolution ○ Supports new solutions SA is interested in ○ Explores innovation opportunities with SA

SAM to Develop Strong Constructive Relationship with Executive Sponsor

Figure 18

Once the sponsors are in place, the strategic account manager is to coordinate the internal engagement activities with the virtual team and the company's executive sponsor, as well as the external activities with the target account. The internal engagement plan would primarily include strategic plan reviews. We delve into the review processes in the next chapter of this book. Further to the reviews, the internal engagement activities should become opportunities to strengthen the executive sponsor's commitment to the role.

As for the external engagement plan, the account manager would be responsible for coordinating the first meetings between target account and firm's executive sponsors; drive the creation of a work agenda, including discussions surrounding collaborative new product development, solutions deployments, possible site visits, and, of course, agree to meetings and reviews rhythm.

CHAPTER SEVEN
Strategic Account Plan Review and Analysis

Strategic Account Management Process

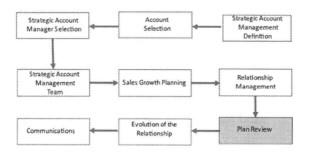

With the planning process completed, including the situational analysis, the growth plan, and the relationship management plan, and the account team focused on executing the strategies and initiatives, it is necessary to periodically review the progress being made. First and foremost, the strategic account manager has the responsibility to monitor progress at the site level. Thus, the account manager must hold periodic internal reviews with the virtual team members to ensure initiatives in the plan are being accomplished. Second, the strategic account manager must engage with the sales team responsible for the pursuit of major projects to understand the progress of the account's project activity and determine ways to utilize influence to drive procurement-selection decisions the company's way. Third, management needs to be satisfied with the level of success the program has attained against the program investment. The abovementioned evaluations are defined as *internal reviews*.

Finally, the strategic account manager, and if nominated and in place the executive sponsor need to encourage the strategic account to hold periodic program performance review meetings to measure the value delivered to both the customer as well as the company. These would be categorized as *external reviews*.

Internal Reviews

Strategic Account Team Reviews

Let's start with the strategic account team reviews. These are to be led by the account manager with the participation of the virtual team members and assigned support staff. The primary evaluation criteria are:

- Reviews with team members are to be site specific
- Reviews are to focus on the site's defensive and offensive initiatives

These reviews may take place on a one-to-one basis with specific site team leaders or may include the whole group for overall evaluation of the strategic account sales growth plan progress. It is the strategic account manager's responsibility to determine the format and frequency of these reviews, although the team reviews should take place at a minimum every month. We recommend that the account manager utilize the tools illustrated in chapter 5, especially those applied to specific sites, when evaluating the plan's progress with each site leader.

Project Activity Reviews

Project activity reviews are conducted by the assigned project sales teams. These reviews are specific to the targeted strategic account capital projects listed in the figure 14. Normally these projects are managed by a separate sales team dedicated to project pursuit, involve a large volume of products and/or services purchases, and thus, are strategic to the company's sales growth goals. Further, the placement of product and services during the capital project phase ensures steady aftermarket business through the maintenance, repair, and operations (MRO) activity taking place post–project startup and commissioning.

Although strategic account managers may have a more consultative role in the project pursuit activity, they can make significant contributions by leveraging the relationships developed with strategic account key individuals able to influence the project's buying decisions. The strategic account manager is well situated to identify project opportunities earlier in the target account's project development process, thus giving the company an opportunity to influence the design to include company products and services before the project moves to the procurement and execution phases. In summary, we recommend the strategic account manager participate in project sales team review meetings to understand the pursuit team's progress and to identify specific activities that may require strategic intervention with the target account.

Management Reviews

When a company commits to and invests in a strategic account program, it is obvious that management will want to ensure that the objectives agreed to during the planning process are being executed within the stipulated timelines. The review process also intends to determine whether the objectives being pursued need adjustment, whether new initiatives are required, and finally, whether the targeted account should be considered for deselection and removal from the program.

The strategic account manager is responsible for preparing the presentation and reporting on the strategic account sales growth plan progress. Generally, the strategic account program's leader, the executive sponsor, and at times one or more virtual team members will be involved and present during the review.

These reviews normally take place with the company's leadership team and with participation by invitation of other individuals, including regional leaders, functional leaders, or other individuals within the organization who may be invited to specific portions of the review. Here are some examples:

- Virtual strategic account team members
- Marketing team members who may be working on specific sales campaigns
- Technical/engineering members interested in learning about target account unmet needs
- New product designers interested in learning more about specific market trends
- Analysts in need of account data to complete specific analyses

The review content may differ from time to time, but in all cases should contain the topics included in figure 19.

Proforma Internal Performance Review Agenda

Participants:
- ○ C-Level representative
- ○ Executive Sponsor
- ○ SAM
- ○ Site leaders
- ○ Sales and marketing management
- ○ Engineering/Design

Typical Agenda

Topic	Presenter
Key accomplishments attained during review period.	SAM
Financial information to date (revenue, gross margin operating income, and corresponding increases or decreases over the previous period)	
Progress report on initiatives being pursued.	
Proposal for initiative adjustments if required.	
Project pursuit progress report.	
Current issues/issue resolution activity	
Critical site activity	
Report on newly discovered unmet needs that can be met with current solutions or met through new product development or new service offerings.	
Share of wallet calculation (annually).	
Relationship status position (annually).	

Figure 19

In most cases, the frequency of these reviews with the leadership team is determined by management. They can take place as frequently as once a quarter but normally on an annual basis. Our experience indicates that the optimal management review schedule is once a year as many initiatives have a long-term timeline. Thus, the need to have sufficient time between reviews to attain levels of progress worth reporting.

External Reviews

Once the relationship between the company and the strategic account reaches a planning-partner level, the strategic account manager should encourage the customer to participate in periodic performance review meetings to evaluate current business levels, review progress made on agreed-on objectives, and initiatives and run postmortem analysis on any issues that have surfaced between review periods. Further, we recommend holding an annual performance review meeting normally led by the company and strategic account executive sponsors. We shall dive into the framework of both types of meetings in more detail.

Periodic Performance Review Meetings (PRM)

The account manager should call for an initial discussion with the strategic account individual responsible for the relationship—normally the appropriate category manager—to agree on the rules of engagement. The rules would include but not be limited to the following:

- Meeting frequency
- Individuals to be involved in the review meetings

- KPIs to be reviewed
- Issues and concerns

Since the intent of the meeting is to increase the intimacy in the relationship with key target account individuals while monitoring your growth progress, we recommend that you hold these reviews on a quarterly basis. Thus, the account manager should encourage the strategic account to have representatives from sourcing and procurement, engineering, and operations functions present if possible.

It is critical that the right key performance indicators be selected to monitor properly the performance of both the company and the customer. The right metrics will consider all areas of importance to both parties. The following are some examples for your consideration:

- Environmental, health, and safety (EHS)
  - o Injury incident rates
  - o Monthly EHS costs
  - o Energy consumption
- Customer satisfaction
  - o On-time delivery
  - o Response time to inquiries
  - o Survey results from users of company's products and/or services
- Quality
  - o First-time pass yields
  - o Mean time between failure
  - o Capacity utilization
- Payment
  - o Customer on-time payment ratio
- Business reviews
  - o Bookings level

- By product
- By site
  - Major projects
  - MRO activities

These quarterly reviews are excellent opportunities to identify and address any issues that may exist with the company's products or services. One of the strategic account manager's core responsibilities is to identify issues and mitigate any risks that are identified.

Annual Performance Review Meetings (APRM)

These reviews are normally led by the company and the account executive sponsors. They provide a higher-level view of the state of the relationship between both firms and are opportunities to identify collaborative activities to improve the performance of the customer's business while increasing the company's sales.

The quarterly reviews provide a foundation for the APRM preparation. A typical APRM agenda is shown in figure 20.

Annual Performance Review

Typical Participants

Strategic Account
Executive Sponsor, Sourcing/Procurement Leader
Operations, Technical/Engineering Leader
Quality Manager

Company
Executive Sponsor, Strategic Account Manager

Topic	Presenter
Safety moment	Company
Industry trends	Strategic Account
Customer state of the business	Strategic Account
Customer challenges and key strategies	Strategic Account
KPI review	Company
Company performance	Company
Issue resolution activity	Company
Company new product development	Company
Innovation and co-creation opportunities review	Strategic Account and Company
Areas of focus to drive cost reduction, improve yields	Strategic Account And Company

Figure 20

It is vitally important to take advantage of the review process to identify any strategic shifts the account may execute due to varying economic cycles or environments. The strategic account manager should be very alert during the strategic planning reviews. He or she should be keen and ready to adjust objectives, goals, and outcomes in accordance with evolving target account strategies due to economic downturns or periods of healthy market growth. As an example, one could mention a situation that occurred during the oil and gas deflationary period starting in late 2014, in which several major oil companies reacted by reducing their headcount in a significant manner, canceling or postponing numerous greenfield projects, and shifting their maintenance strategy from predictive and/or preventative guidelines to a run-to-fail mode. Such a shift in customer strategies calls for a corresponding shift in the company's initiatives. Following you will find an example of our shift in strategy with an oil and gas account.

This particular account reacted quickly to the deflation of the price of crude oil by reducing headcount in a significant manner, leaving its asset management and administration of its equipment maintenance program without a leader. Our strategic account manager identified this sudden gap and immediately contacted the account's maintenance and service director with an offer to backfill the gap with our own embedded resources. Since we had prior knowledge of their equipment-installed base, systems, and procedures, the strategic account found our proposal to be an ideal alternative to contracting a service organization to backfill the aforementioned gap.

In addition to reviewing the information covered during the quarterly meetings, the annual performance review meeting should focus on the target account's positioning based on its industry's trends, its concerns, and its strategies. The strategic account executive sponsor would also be interested in the company's near and long-term plans related to new product development and service offerings. The company should seek to marry its portfolio of existing and new solutions to meet the customer's soon-to-be-implemented strategies and objectives. Furthermore, the company should attempt to identify opportunities to cocreate solutions that would benefit the customer's business performance. These cocreation opportunities would include but not be limited to product design, embedded application engineering support, pilot programs, and beta testing. We delve into these in more detail in the next chapter.

CHAPTER EIGHT
Evolution of the Strategic Account Relationship

Strategic Account Management Process

By now you should realize that two key components of a successful account management strategy involve proper segmentation and subsequent selection of the right companies to be included in the program. The relationship status scale, as well as the selection matrix, are two of the tools we recommend you use to decide how to segment your customer base. Once you select the accounts to be included in the top-tier level (strategic accounts), you will be making decisions on the resources assigned to each strategic account as well as the level of value to be delivered.

Depending on the relationship status you have with each strategic account, as well as the scoring attained through the selection matrix, you may consider segmenting the top tier into additional levels with increased value proposition delivery mechanisms. We suggest considering a silver-gold-platinum (Ag-Au-Pt) structure. The intention of this additional segmentation is to motivate strategic accounts to seek a more profound relationship with your company and drive for greater value of products and services rendered. In short, to commit to a partnering status with your firm.

As the strategic account climbs the Ag-Au-Pt ladder, it receives greater levels of value that may be delivered through numerous means. It is the responsibility of the strategic account management program leader as well as the company's leadership team to determine the different value propositions to be delivered at each level. Clearly the higher the level, the greater the amount of value delivered to the account.

Concurrently, the Ag-Au-Pt program must ensure that while the target account attains more value the higher it is positioned, your company is also winning through increased volume of business, higher overall profitability, improved and more balanced product and/or service portfolio placement, and in short, greater share of wallet.

The following are a few examples of value that could be packaged into each tier:

- Access to technical resources not available to lower status customers
- Additional aftermarket services
- Extended warranties
- Lower overall cost per unit

- Dedicated customer support resources
- Preferred delivery terms
- Extended payment terms
- Asset management resources
- Dedicated emergency phone line
- Dedicated Web portal for accessing pricing, documentation, drawings, etc.
- Co-creation investment opportunities

Please refer to the example shown in figure 21 for reference only.

Value	Silver	Gold	Platinum
SA discount level A			✓
SA discount level B		✓	
SA discount Level C	✓		
Extended warranty		✓	✓
Extended payment terms			✓
Direct access to technical staff		✓	✓
Dedicated customer support resources		✓	✓
Preferred delivery terms	✓	✓	✓
Dedicated emergency contact access - phone/email/app			✓
Dedicated web portal – pricing, delivery, documentation		✓	✓
Asset management/monitoring services	✓	✓	✓
Tailor made aftermarket services			✓
Co –creation investments			✓

Figure 21

Once the Ag-Au-Pt program is created, it must be marketed and sold internally and externally. We recommend that you engage with your marketing team to create the marketing collateral required to successfully promote the program.

Partnering with the Strategic Account

The relationship a company develops with strategic accounts should strengthen over time, reaching planning-partner and ideally trusted-adviser statuses. It is by reaching these levels in the relationship that the company can insert itself in the customer's planning process and have greater leverage with the customer's supplier selections. In fact, once a company develops the intimacy and trust atmosphere attained by reaching trusted-adviser status with the strategic account, it is well situated to drive partnering initiatives that can significantly benefit the strategic account's business while increasing sales and profitability. Clearly, we are referring to those accounts classified in the platinum tier.

So, what does partnering with your customer actually mean? The *Business Dictionary* offers the following definition:

> Establishing a long-term win-win relationship based on mutual trust and teamwork, and on sharing of both risks and rewards. The objective is to focus on what each party does best, by sharing financial and other resources, and establishing specific roles for each participant.

It is the responsibility of the account manager, and to a degree the executive sponsor, to initiate discussions with key individuals within the strategic account's organization to uncover concerns that limit the ability to make business improvements as these concerns may trigger partnering opportunities. The strategic account manager should drive these conversations by touching on multiple areas, including but not limited to the following:

- Health and environmental safety
- Efficiencies/yields
- On-time delivery to strategic account customers
- Cost reduction
- Quality
- Technical/engineering
- Digital transformation/industrial internet of things (IIoT)
- Profitability
- Business/sales growth

Strategic account managers must command business savvy competence when having these discussions as they must identify, sort, and present to management any partnering opportunities deriving from the abovementioned conversations with the strategic account. Our experience indicates that the areas of collaboration may be vast. We shall delve into a few examples for illustration purposes.

Embedded Resources

Strategic accounts currently evaluate their human resource assets on a continuous basis, seeking to focus on functions that correspond to the firm's core competences. Noncore, specialized, or very technical activities with shortages of human resources are examined and considered for outsourcing. However, due to the critical nature of these activities, the number of suppliers to be considered is reduced. If your company has the right human resources to satisfy the target account's technical needs, you may leverage your relationship status and seek a partnering arrangement for the supply of these critical resources at a competitive cost.

The customer wins by having trustworthy personnel perform critical functions at below-market prices. The company wins by inserting contracted specialists within the strategic account's organization and thus, being well situated to uncover additional unmet needs that could be supplied by the company.

Asset Leasing

Strategic accounts may have internal budgeting issues limiting capital expense funds. The account manager may assist the strategic account by offering leasing arrangements for the capital equipment required, thus bypassing the budget approval process. The leasing arrangement may be limited to the asset or may include complete maintenance and repair services as well.

The customer wins by obtaining the equipment sooner. The company wins by placing the equipment in the customer's plant, ensuring a steady aftermarket business.

New Product Development and Testing

Your company may be developing a new product that is targeted to the strategic account's industry segment. All in-house testing is completed, but no external evaluations or field testing has taken place. Due to the critical service the new product is to address, it becomes difficult to find customer locations to perform beta testing (real case scenario testing at an actual processing location). The strategic account manager may leverage the relationship and knowledge of the target account's network to find locations that are willing to test the new equipment in a critical service.

The customer wins as it would be involved in the final stages of the product development, would have a say in its final design to fit its specific needs, and could be the first to realize benefits and value the new product may deliver to customers within its industry segment. The company wins as it expedites the launching of this new product with proven field performance.

Cocreation Opportunities

The strategic account may be developing a new technology or business process requiring either a product or service not yet available in the marketplace. The strategic account manager should identify this need as an opportunity to cocreate such a product and/or service and drive efforts to secure agreements related to the development process, intellectual property rights, confidentiality terms, investment responsibilities from both parties, commercial terms, and selling and profit rights. Successful cocreation deals require a high level of trust on the part of both parties as the initial investment in funds as well as human resources and time is significant.

The strategic account wins as the cocreated product is tailor-made for the new process or technology being designed. The company wins as the target account's unmet need can now be exclusively satisfied by the cocreated product.

Please be aware that the abovementioned partnering examples are neither novel nor unique ideas of the authors. However, our experience indicates that these potential opportunities do not prosper unless an extraordinarily strong and intimate relationship exists between both parties. This level of relationship is incredibly difficult to reach without having a sound strategic account management program in place.

CHAPTER NINE
Program Communications

Strategic Account Management Process

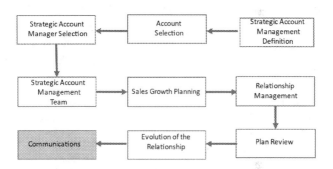

One of the definitions of a program is "a plan of procedure." To that end, it is very important to create a strategy to communicate the plan and the plan's results internally within the company and externally with the strategic account. Without a robust and well-executed communication strategy, neither the expectations of the program nor the results of the program will be clear. This can lead to apathy toward the entire program, evolving to an overall lack of support by both the company as well as the strategic account. Let's look at ways of communicating the plan and the results internally and externally.

Internal Communication

Because strategic account teams are quite different from the day-to-day sales organization, it is particularly important to use effective ways to communicate progress and successes as they take place. Day-to-day sales teams are evaluated at least monthly as finance reports order intake by region or sales district. Depending on the ERP systems or systems that a company uses, getting global order intake by strategic account on a regular basis may be very difficult if not impossible. Therefore, it is particularly important that the strategic account organization creates innovative and effective ways to let the internal organization understand the strategic account plan and the progress that is being made throughout the year related to its execution. We talked earlier about the need to get input from the virtual sales team as the strategic account plan is constructed. Input will be required from some of the site leaders, especially for those sites that are deemed critical to the growth of the business with the account. But it is imperative that once the plan is complete, each site team leader understands the major initiatives and strategies that are part of the plan. This can best be communicated by a conference call or video meeting, where the strategic account manager prepares a presentation to highlight the key parts of the strategic account plan. Depending on the level of interest at the executive level, a separate call with the company president and CFO might make sense as well.

If your company has a robust CRM system in place, it can be used very effectively to help keep the entire virtual team up to date on what is happening at the account's corporate headquarters as well as activity taking place at each global site. It is necessary to make sure that the account team has access to all account records associated with the specific strategic account in order for this to be effective.

Throughout the year, it is especially important to tell the story related to progress and particularly successes with each account. There are several suggested ways to do this.

First, one method is to have each strategic account manager prepare a monthly report. This report can be structured in various ways, but it should focus on progress made that month with her or his account(s). If the business is organized around business units, it might help to focus on successes by business unit so that the business unit leaders only need to focus on the information related to their units. If the decision is made to produce monthly reports, it is important that each account manager follow the same format. Creating a template is helpful in this regard. It is also important that the reports are sent out in a timely manner, so they are relevant when they are read. A distribution list should also be created to make sure they get sent to all in the organization who might be interested. An example of a monthly report template is included in the appendix.

In addition to monthly reports, some strategic account organizations create a periodic newsletter that covers topics related to the entire strategic account program. These articles could be related to personnel changes on the team or changes to the overall program. They could be specific to a strategic account. Specific account articles could cover a multitude of topics. Some examples are:

- Important meetings with strategic accounts
- Major agreements signed with strategic accounts

- Acquisitions made by strategic accounts
- Major project wins with strategic accounts
- Strategic accounts being added to the program

Unlike the monthly reports that can easily be submitted with a simple template, we encourage the strategic account team to engage with the marketing communications department to create a professional-looking document. That way the newsletter will not only provide important information to the organization related to the strategic accounts, it will also show the reader the level of professionalism within the strategic account team. An example of the opening of a strategic account newsletter can be found in the appendix.

External Communication

Communication with the strategic account was covered further in chapter 7. However, it may be helpful to leverage marketing communications to develop collateral to effectively communicate with the strategic account. The following are some examples for reference:

- Brochures explaining and detailing contracts between the strategic account and the company
- Flyers announcing important agreements between the two companies
- Account-specific catalogs detailing products and services available to the strategic account
- Announcements about past or upcoming meetings between the strategic account and the company

In addition to collateral specific to the strategic account, such as the examples above, it may be helpful to develop a brochure that explains the benefits of the overall strategic account program so prospective strategic accounts understand why it would be good to be part of the program.

We should not underestimate the importance of the performance review meetings detailed in chapter 7. These quarterly and annual reviews with the strategic account are opportunities to strengthen relationships with it, communicate the value your firm adds to the customer's operation, and identify any concerns and/or threats your company may have to face in the future.

Clearly there are other ways to communicate both internally and externally about the progress being made with a specific account and with the overall program. The key is to decide how you will communicate and then execute that plan consistently. It is important that stakeholders both within the company and at the strategic account understand what to expect in the way of information. Regardless, too much communication is always better than delivering insufficient information.

CHAPTER TEN
Lessons Learned

As mentioned in the preface, we experienced several setbacks that created lessons learned. We feel we should share some of these with those who are embarking on a strategic account program in order to be prepared should they encounter the same challenges.

Lesson 1: Be Aware of Logistics and Culture When Selecting Account Leaders

When we first started our program, we identified, rated, and ultimately selected a strategic account with specific language and cultural traits. We proceeded to search for a strategic account manager both internally and externally. The search proved difficult as we had trouble identifying a candidate who had the business acumen, cultural and language skills, and was located close to the account headquarters and engineering center. Instead of continuing the search, we opted to assign an account leader who did not meet all the requirements. More specifically, the person selected did not have an appreciation of the account's cultural traits. Our rush to fill this position with the less-than-optimal candidate resulted in making little to no progress with the account.

Lesson 2: Select Account Leaders Who Are Strong Business Leaders, not Just Great "Elephant Hunters"

We had an account leader assigned to an important strategic account who knew that account very well, understood our product offering, and was an excellent salesperson. However, the account leader struggled with crucial strategic objectives including planning activities, account reviews, and performance reviews with management. The result still delivered growth rates above the percentage growth attained from standard accounts primarily due to the account leader's rainmaking tremendous sales capabilities. However, the level of growth was inconsistent, and the relationship with the leadership team deteriorated over time due to the account leader's lack of organizational skills, planning, and political savvy when dealing with the company's top management team. As a result, it was necessary to assign another strategic account leader to the account; this one had stronger administrative skills. We kept the original account leader on the account, focusing his responsibilities on the sales function as his skills in this area were critical. But he reported directly to the newly appointed account leader.

Lesson 3: Make Sure You Have Executive-Level Support of Your Program

We found that when a change in leadership occurred we needed to resell the strategic account program. During one of the leadership team changes we were not able to convince our new president of the importance of the strategic account program, that it needed to be an enterprise-wide imperative, not just a sales initiative. Furthermore, the new leadership team was not fully committed to the program. Therefore, the contribution from different areas of the organization was difficult to obtain resulting in nonvalue-added internal negotiating efforts with different business functions for support including finance, engineering, and product management. As a result, we struggled with the execution of our strategic plans and experienced delays in attaining results. Below are several areas where we struggled as a result of not having support at the executive level.

- Our ability to obtain regular financial information was greatly compromised
- We experienced resistance from manufacturing to prioritize strategic account orders
- Product management demonstrated a lack of interest in participating in cocreated new product development programs with strategic accounts

Lesson 4: Have the Leader of the Strategic Account Program Report to the President of the Business, not the Company Sales Leader

During our time running our strategic account program, we had several reporting structures. We found that our program was most successful when we reported to the president of the business rather than the overall sales leader. The sales function requires a focus on immediate results, such as month end, quarter end, and annual bookings and sales. We like to use the following analogy. The sales department is responsible for "bringing home the bacon" to feed the organization on a daily basis. The strategic account management program is not merely part of the sales function; it is a business-wide function that looks at longer-term objectives including, but not limited to the following results:

- Sales growth greater than that of standard accounts over time
- Increased profitability over time
- Strong relationships with strategic accounts
- Widening of our product portfolio through cocreation activities

As indicated in chapter 3, the program needs to be an enterprise-wide initiative to be most successful. Thus, having the overall strategic account program leader report to the leadership team and not the sales function sets the tone throughout the organization.

Lesson 5: Strategic Account Program KPIs Must Be a Part of Every Virtual Team Member's Incentive Plan

We struggled in this area as regional sales leaders decided on the objectives and goals as well as the metrics on which the salespeople under them would be measured. So, in many cases, strategic account managers had to lead without authority as well as without a reward mechanism to call virtual sales team members into action. In short, a most successful strategic account program requires that virtual team members be properly incentivized to drive the specific activities and initiatives assigned to the location they cover.

Conclusion

We trust that after reading the preceding chapters you understand the benefits a strategic account program can provide to your business. Strategic accounts are significant company assets that need to be nurtured, developed, and protected. Furthermore, the globalization trends that have taken place at the turn of the twenty-first century have forced companies to reinvent the way they organize their sales efforts as customers' major procurement decisions are no longer made at the local or regional levels; they are made and executed globally. Interaction with customers' corporate management teams, potentially including their C-suite officials, is crucial to successful sales growth plans. The art of sales has become significantly more complex. Companies will cease to flourish unless they address their key customers' evolving procurement practices and adjust their sales organizations accordingly. In short, a strategic account management program should not be viewed as a sales organizational initiative. For the program to be successful it must be considered an enterprise-wide imperative and have the full commitment of the company's leadership team.

A crucial first step in the creation of a strategic account management program involves the proper sizing and selection of the accounts. Remember, smaller here is better than bigger. The selection process requires that the right criteria and its appropriate weighting be used. We recommend you utilize the scoring tool included in the appendix as your guide.

Once the accounts have been selected, the company needs to commit to the deployment of the right resources to grow the business at a significantly higher rate compared to other accounts. The selection of the right account managers becomes a paramount endeavor in the process. The strategic account manager is not just a salesperson. The manager must first and foremost be a businessperson capable of discerning customer challenges, concerns, strategies, and objectives. The manager must also be capable of finding solutions to ease said concerns and support their growth and profitability objectives. The strategic account manager must excel at numerous core competences in order to be successful. Please refer to the sample job description included in the appendix for more details.

Strategic account management resources may be identified within the organization or recruited externally depending on the talent levels available internally as well as human resources strategies the organization may have in place for high-potential individuals. At the end of the day, the individual selected is to become the company's relationship manager, business developer, and driver of long-term revenue and profitability growth with the strategic account.

As indicated before, the strategic account management program must be embraced from an enterprise-wide perspective. The account manager requires access to other resources not necessarily dedicated 100 percent to this effort. But when needed, they must be available and committed to performing the tasks required to ensure total customer satisfaction and as a result, drive the growth rates expected from the strategic account. This group of human resources collectively becomes what we call the *virtual team*. The team is to be led by the strategic account manager and is responsible for driving forward the objectives delineated in the account plan.

To maximize the level of success with a strategic account, the account manager must create and execute a well-prepared account sales plan. The account plan should start with an analysis of the situation before setting initiatives, goals, and objectives. The plan should include the following:

1. Situational analysis
   a. Strategic account business analysis
   b. Competitive landscape and analysis
   c. Company position with the strategic account
2. Sales growth plan
   a. Defensive initiatives
   b. Offensive initiatives
   c. Capital project pursuit
   d. Business growth objectives and impact

One may have the best plan in place, but the key to success is founded on the efficient execution of said plan. This cannot be accomplished unless a sound relationship management plan is developed and put in place. The strategic account manager and virtual team must know and have strong ties with the right individuals within the target account organization that either make the procurement decisions or can significantly influence them. After all, these individuals ultimately will be responsible for the success or failure of the strategic account manager's sales growth plan.

As your company climbs the relationship status ladder, there may come a time when the executive sponsor should be introduced to the strategic account. The executive sponsor should preferably be part of the company's leadership team and has the following responsibilities:

- Becomes the account's advocate within the company's leadership team
- Commits to attend annual performance review meetings
- Mentors and guides the strategic account manager
- Is open and responsive to major issue resolution
- Supports new solutions in which the strategic account is interested
- Explores innovation opportunities with the strategic account

Once the sales plan is in place, the account manager should perform periodic reviews as follows:

1. Internal reviews
   a. Reviews with the virtual team
   b. Project reviews
   c. Management reviews
2. External reviews with the strategic account
   a. PRMs
   b. APRMs

The purpose of the internal review with the virtual team is to measure the progress made compared to the plan objectives, determine if changes to the plan are required, and ensure that the team remains engaged and committed. Furthermore, internal team reviews should include deep dives into the specific site-based account plans.

The intent of the management reviews is to present the level of progress achieved to the company's leadership team, present any plan adjustments that may be required to secure the results forecasted in the account plan, and in short, validate the investment made in the strategic account program.

External reviews become more and more relevant as the company's relationship status increases. These reviews intend to present key performance indicator results versus the mutually set targets, ensure the account that the objectives agreed to are met, and brainstorm opportunities that may add value to both the strategic account as well as the company. Normally the annual performance reviews involve the participation of the company's assigned executive sponsor as well as the strategic account executive responsible for the relationship development with your firm.

As your strategic account management program matures, you may consider further segmenting the strategic account base with specific and increased value delivery mechanisms. We propose a silver, gold, and platinum structure. Refer to the example depicted in figure 21 in chapter 8 for details.

A robust and well-executed communication strategy is necessary to have a successful strategic account program. It is important that the strategic account team work with the marketing department to create effective ways to communicate both internally and externally about progress being made relative to the strategic account plan.

We hope our final chapter on lessons learned helps you avoid some of the pitfalls that we encountered as we tried to move our overall program forward. A well-run strategic account program can provide significant benefits to both your company and your strategic accounts. Our hope is that this handbook has provided you with valuable information that can help you build and execute your own program.

Appendix

Definition of Acronyms

Acronym	Definition
Ag-Au-Pt	silver-gold-platinum
APRM	annual performance review meeting
B2B	business to business
Beta testing	real case scenario testing at a manufacturing or processing location
CAGR	compounded annual growth rate
C-level	executive level in an organization
CRM	customer relationship management
EHS	environmental, health, and safety
IIoT	industrial internet of things
IT	information technology
KPI	key performance indicator
M&A	mergers and acquisitions
MRO	maintenance, repair, and operation
OTD	on-time delivery
PRM	performance review meeting
R&D	research and development
SA	strategic account
SAM	strategic account manager
SAMA	Strategic Account Management Association
SWOT	strengths, weaknesses, opportunities, threats
VP	vice president

Selection Matrix

Potential Strategic Account	XYZ			
Selection Criteria	Selection Weight	Account Score	Account Criteria Scores	Scoring Criteria
Global Presence	20	3	60	Presence in One Region=1 Presence in Two Regions=3, Presence in Three Regions=5
Current Revenue	25	5	125	<1MM Revenue=1, 1-5MM=3, >5MM =5
Current Profitability	25	5	125	<20% GM=1, 20-25% GM=3, >25% GM=5
Account Leadership	15	3	45	Industry Follower=1, Industry Leader=3, Strong Industry Leader=5
Interest in a Partnering Relationship	15	3	45	Little Interest=1, Some Interest=3, Strong Interest in Partnering=5
Overall Account Score	100		400	

Global Account Selection Committee

Functions	Strategy & Marketing	Sales	Service	Manufacturing	Engineering	Finance
Key stakeholders	• Director M&A and Strat	• VP Sales • Global Accounts Director	• VP Service	• Manufacturing Leader	• VP Engineering	• CFO
Required Input	• Potential Global Accounts scoring according to pre-defined selection and deselection criteria	• Qualitative assessment related to ease of business	• Qualitative assessment related to service opportunities	• Global product availability	• Co-creation & NPD opportunities	• Account revenue and profitability

Strategic Account Manager Operating Rhythm

While operating rhythm for a strategic account manager is quite individual, here we provide suggested activities and the frequency within which we recommend they take place.

Weekly
- Strategic account team meetings/calls
- Meeting with program manager

Monthly
- Submission of monthly reports
- Meeting with executive sponsor

Quarterly
- Meeting with virtual team, including all site team leaders
- Submission of articles for the strategic account newsletter

Biannually
- Meeting with strategic account
- Update meeting with executive sponsor and executive team
- Update strategic plan, including the account status within the program

Annually
- Development of strategic plan
- Annual meeting with strategic account

- Annual update meeting with executive sponsor and executive team
- Update status of account related to account status within the program

Sample Job Description:
Global Strategic Account Manager

	Global Strategic Account Manager (SAM)
Job Title	
Job Code	
Business Unit/BU	
Reports to	Director, Strategic Account Management Program

Summary of Role

The primary role of the strategic account manager (SAM) is to support the realization of the corporate account plan within the assigned strategic account and facilitate growth of the business unit product and services with the strategic account. The SAM participates as a core sales team member and leader of the virtual team. The SAM defines the strategic business drivers for an account, drives the initiatives, and aligns BU resources. The objective is to position the company and the BU as the primary supplier by the account. The job requires deep knowledge of the industry and application as well as how to apply the BU's technology, products, and services optimally. The job requires deep knowledge of the BU's key players at headquarters, across functions, and across the globe.

Principal Job Responsibilities

- Acts as the single point of leadership and voice of the BU and its entire portfolio of capabilities, technology, products, and services within the strategic account core team.
- Acts as single point of contact for the strategic account core team to navigate the BU across functions and/or world regions.
- Develops integrated structured programs that enable successful achievement of the customers' strategic business initiatives.
- Captures and rolls up success stories and proven and qualified results.
- Acts as a coach/mentor for the global account team to named critical or secondary sites, site team leaders, and/or site teams.
- Communicates BU's strategic programs to assigned strategic accounts.
- Ensures the full scope of supply for the BU is in play on project pursuits.
- Working in a team environment, develops and proactively executes the BU's business plans for assigned strategic accounts.

1. Voice of the Company

- Identifies and helps drive ideas to make the BU easier to do business with.
- Understands the current business conditions, active projects (in all project phases), buying processes,

competition, suppliers, and organizational structures for each assigned strategic account.

- Supplies account metrics and KPIs specific to the BU to the account team.
- Organizes for business strategy reviews and visitations by the strategic account to BU offices and factories.
- Keeps the account team informed of new capabilities and road maps for introduction of these and pushes for opportunities to communicate these plans to the account.
- Supports the company's sales model in attaining and developing sales collateral, such as referrals for the platforms of the BU.
- Organizes for the collaboration of presentations with members of the account at industry forums.
- Pushes for changes to the portfolio that will contribute to greater customer satisfaction and contribute to growth in sales from the account.

2. Sales Planning and Execution

- Responsible for developing and driving a global plan that delivers profitable sales growth at a specific account.
- Ensures alignment and synergy occur with the strategic account team.
- Ensures that the top global projects are being appropriately managed and pursued, and communications are occurring.
- Pursues AML/AVL approval/acceptance for all BU products and services.

- Establishes high-level contacts and relationships on the BU's behalf at the strategic account
- Tracks account's buying behavior, pricing history, and spending with the BU
- Communicates account performance to BU management
- Contributes understanding of the assigned account's vendor status for platforms sold by the BU
- Furnishes information for sales order forecasting processes
- Functions as the BU focal point for input to commercial T&Cs and pricing on agreements, and leads pricing and T&C development on behalf of the BU in agreement formation
- Drives frame agreements when applicable
- Contributes pricing recommendations for projects and agreements based on factual observations of pricing in the account's industry and prior history with the account
- Ensures that new product development needs of global accounts are communicated to the appropriate personnel within the organization

3. Global Project Pursuit

- Identifies and selects projects in which the BU will participate and drives a coordinated pursuit, communication, and tracking strategy for each project globally
- Facilitates the resourcing of global project pursuits and facilitates assignment of a BU sales lead on all select global projects

- Acts as the liaison for specific account opportunities with the project pursuit team on a regular basis
- Assists in proposal development by helping secure BU resources for product quotations' and services' estimation as well as narrates the value propositions that resonate with the account
- Provides input and guidance on strategic pricing for project opportunities when applicable
- Works with the sales team to position BU's portfolio earlier in the project cycle to achieve maximum company content
- Fosters global project communication and utilizes BU resources to win select projects
- Reviews project lists for assigned strategic accounts and coordinates resources
- Reviews project pipeline regularly to ensure accuracy and completeness
- Supports project pursuit and execution efforts within Dynamic's Engineering Centers

Required Core Competences

Personal	Professional	Management/ Leadership
Customer-focused Business acumen Presentation skills Interpersonal savvy Communication skills Integrity, ethics, and trust Perseverance Teamwork Motivational Listens to others Manages diversity Personal learning	Solution/consultative selling BU-wide sales processes BU-wide portfolio Knowledge of BU operations, processes Business, financial negotiation **Strategic Skills** Learning on the fly Managing vision and purpose Dealing with ambiguity Strategic mindset	Strategic vision Organization agility Action-oriented Drive for results Building effective winning teams Prioritizing, planning, and organizing Influence without direct authority Comfort around higher management Political savvy

Required Qualifications and Experience

Qualified candidates must possess a BS in business, engineering, or a technical field, and have at least seven years of sales leadership, account management experience, or related industry marketing experience in the industry of the account. Candidates need to have proven ability to develop and implement strategic plans and demonstrate business acumen and strong drive for results. Furthermore, candidates need to be self-starters with enough knowledge of the BU's capabilities and who and how things get done to navigate the formal and informal channels of the BU and the process group.

Sample Job Description: Global Strategic Account Program Manager

Department/Location: Global strategic accounts
Reports to: Director, global strategic accounts
Date Posted: XX/XX/XXXX

Job Summary:

Reporting to the director, global strategic accounts, the global strategic account program manager will be responsible for leading the effort and managing the development, organization, standardization, and implementation of high-scale projects and associated sales tools and data to support the overall account program within Dynamic Corporation.

To that end, the successful individual will be strongly aligned with CRM and GSA programs and initiatives, providing strategic input and overall project management support to the global account team.

The program manager will achieve improved efficiencies through support and organization that enable the GSA organization to demonstrate significant value to the largest and most important accounts globally, increase customer-installed base, and overall improved margins and productivity.

Major Responsibilities

- Work with the global account managers and directors, assisting in the development of strategic objectives for the assigned accounts
- Be the key interface with site team leaders and global account managers and directors
- Assist and lead the account managers to mitigate program risks
- Supervise work execution and manage core data obtained from the BU for collation
- Facilitate regular reporting to the GSA team using performance reports issued by the BUs
- Facilitate BU leader updates to senior executive stakeholders at the VP level
- Develop and structure comprehensive and professional global proposals and agreements with the account leaders, global account managers, and directors for key accounts
  - Support data integrity for large and special projects and agreements.
  - Provide data analysis and integrity checks within the GSA team.
- Provide strategic guidance to the site teams and coordinate the management of the BU sales teams, facilitating the collection of information required for RFIs
- Provide strategic input to aid the development and standardization of applied GSA management processes and sales tools (including, but not limited to selection tools, quotation tools, and data analysis tools), ensuring these are fully optimized to suit each key account

- Jointly develop and execute contract roll-out solutions with global account managers, directors, and account leaders to ensure effective implementation and provide support to the sales operations relative to GSA customers

Reporting:

Program manager reports to the director, global strategic accounts and liaises closely with global strategic managers and directors for each assigned account to:

- Provide regular reports to GSA directors including, but not limited to:
    o Maintaining the account plan, ensuring this reflects biannual status
    o Site team initiatives
    o BU performance reports
    o Sales figures and bookings updates
    o GSA growth initiatives
    o GSA project dashboards and scorecards

Preferred Skills and Experience:

- Bachelor's degree in marketing/business management, finance, or a technical/engineering discipline at an advanced level preferred
- Financially oriented with exceptional business judgment and exposure to commercial and/or marketing functions

- Excellent planning and organizational skills with strong analytical and problem-solving acumen
- Proven track record of managing project work with exposure to the EPC contractor community
- Excellent MS Office skills, in particular Excel, Access, and Word
- Experience in process improvement initiatives and practices
- Good interpersonal skills and ability to work with multiple levels of management and across different functional areas
- Successful track record within a dynamic, growth-oriented organization
- Willing to travel (approximately 10 to 20 percent of the time)

Core Competencies:

- Business acumen
- Customer focus
- Decision quality
- Drive for results
- Integrity and trust
- Project management
- Strategic agility

Critical Site List

Critical Site List						
Customer Critical Site Name	**Virtual Team Member Assigned to Site**	**Relationship Status with Site's Management**	**Installed Base**			
			Product 1	**Product 2**	**Product 3**	**Product 4**

Relationship Status Scale	Installed Base Scale
1—Vendor	1—Low (less than 10%)
2—Preferred vendor	2—Moderate (10–40%)
3—Planning partner	3—High (40 %+)
4—Trusted adviser	

Customer Strategies and
Enabling Solutions

Customer Strategies and Enabling Solutions				
	Customer Strategies			
Customer Initiatives	**Strategy 1**	**Strategy 2**	**Strategy 3**	**Strategy 4**
Initiative 1				
Initiative 2				
Initiative 3				
Initiative 4				
Company Enablers	**Company Solutions**	**Company Solutions**	**Company Solutions**	**Company Solutions**
Solution 1				
Solution 2				
Solution 3				
Solution 4				

Sample SWOT Analysis Chart (for Strategic Account and for Company)

SWOT ANALYSIS

For Strategic Account ▨
For Company ☐

Strengths	Weaknesses

Opportunities	Threats

Key insights:

Competitive Matrix Tool

Competitive Matrix

Product Group:	Customer:			Scores		
Rating Related to	Buying Decision Factor Importance	Weighting	Your Company	Competitor 1	Competitor 2	Competitor 3
Product	Quality	5				
	Price	4				
	Delivery	3				
	Fit for purpose	2				
Company	Ease of doing business	5				
	Global footprint	4				
	Aftermarket support	3				
	Innovation capability	2				
Sales Team	Technical knowledge	5				
	Availability	4				
	Responsiveness	3				
Totals						

Product Portfolio Status

Product Portfolio Status			
Customer:	**Status**		
Product/Service	**None**	**Acceptable**	**Preferred**

Key Insights:

Offering Potential Matrix

Offering Potential Matrix						
Customer:	Product 1		Product 2		Product 3	
Customer Initiatives/ Concerns	Rating	Comments	Rating	Comments	Rating	Comments

Rating Scale:

1—Low potential

2—Moderate potential.

3—High potential

Overall Business Growth Chart

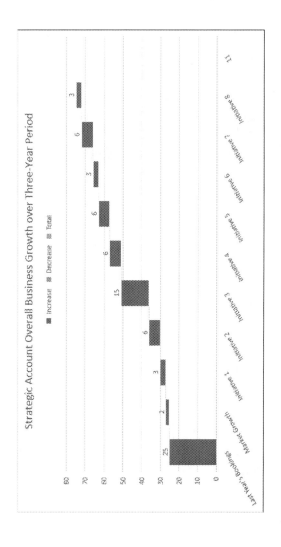

Strategic Account Overall Business Growth over Three-Year Period

■ Increase ■ Decrease ■ Total

Relationship Assessment
and Management Plan

Customer:								
Individual Name	**Title and Role**	**Buying Decision Responsibility**	**Attitude Toward Company**	**Individual Professional Drivers/Needs**	**Individual Personal Drivers/Needs**	**Who in Our Team Is Aligned with This Individual?**	**Actions to Grow Relationship**	

Relationship Assessment and Management Plan

Title and Role Scale	Buying Decision Responsibility Scale	Attitude w/ Company Scale
Finance	Approver	Advocate
Procurement	Decision-Maker	Supporter
Technical	Recommender	Neutral
Operations	Influencer	Blocker
Engineering	Other	
Other		

Relationship Status Scale

Company Relationship Status Scale	
Trusted Adviser	☐
Planning Partner	☐
Preferred Vendor	☐
Vendor	☐

Executive Sponsor Selection and Pairing Tool

Executive Sponsor Selection and Pairing Tool		
Traits	**Potential SA Executive**	**Potential Company Executive**
Education		
Languages		
Work History		
Product Knowledge		
Industry Knowledge		
Personality		
Hobbies		
Sports		
Availability		

Sample Value Delivery Program

Value	Silver	Gold	Platinum
SA discount level A			✓
SA discount level B		✓	
SA discount Level C	✓		
Extended warranty		✓	✓
Extended payment terms			✓
Direct access to technical staff		✓	✓
Dedicated customer support resources		✓	✓
Preferred delivery terms	✓	✓	✓
Dedicated emergency contact access - phone/email/app			✓
Dedicated web portal – pricing, delivery, documentation		✓	✓
Asset management/monitoring services	✓	✓	✓
Tailor made aftermarket services			✓
Co –creation investments			✓

Sample Newsletter

Q1 Global Account Newsletter

Greetings to All from the Dynamics Global Account Team!

We are still in the process of finalizing our bookings results for Q1 for our global accounts. The preliminary numbers indicate that, on aggregate, bookings grew slightly in Q1 despite significant headwinds experienced by many of our very important customers. We enjoyed nice project orders from Customer 1, Customer 2, and Customer 3. However, the continued impact of the low oil prices has forced some of our global accounts to cancel or postpone capital projects and further reduce MRO spending. Despite this, we continue to better position ourselves for the future by increasing our AML listings and discussing with our global accounts solutions such as the ABC product. Below you will find articles related to progress and success with our global accounts in the first quarter.

Best regards,
Jill Simpson

Sample Global Strategic Account Manager Monthly Report

Strategic Account Manager: **Date:**

Program Manager:

Business Pulse:

Significant Activity / Successes of Note:

Cross-Business Unit Activity

Business Unit 1

Business Unit 2

Business Unit 3

Major Obstacles/Issues:

Next Month's Objectives:

Index

Printed in the United States
by Baker & Taylor Publisher Services